– THE –
DISAPPEARED

THE CLEVELAND KIDNAPPINGS
AND OTHER SHOCKING CASES

AL CIMINO

D0061345

JOHN BLAKE

Published by John Blake Publishing Ltd,
3 Bramber Court, 2 Bramber Road,
London W14 9PB, England

www.johnblakepublishing.co.uk

www.facebook.com/Johnblakepub facebook
twitter.com/johnblakepub twitter

First published in paperback in 2014

ISBN: 978-1-78219-901-4

British Library Cataloguing-in-Publication Data:

A catalogue record for this book is available from the British Library.

Design by www.envydesign.co.uk

Printed in Great Britain by CPI Group (UK) Ltd

1 3 5 7 9 10 8 6 4 2

Papers used by John Blake Publishing are natural, recyclable products made
from wood grown in sustainable forests. The manufacturing processes conform
to the environmental regulations of the country of origin.

– THE –
DISAPPEARED

CONTENTS

PART II - MORE MISSING AMERICANS

PART III - INTERNATIONAL ABDUCTION

INTRODUCTION

When the news broke that three women had been held captive for over ten years in Cleveland, Ohio, the world was shocked. It seemed unbelievable that they could have been kept prisoner in a seemingly normal house by a man well known in the community just a few blocks from where they had disappeared. Neighbours and friends had spotted nothing and no one suspected their captor, Ariel Castro, of being a depraved monster who used the young girls as sex slaves while simultaneously maltreating and torturing them.

Sadly, America and the world had been shocked before. How could Jaycee Lee Dugard have been held for 18 years in the back garden of convicted sex offender David Garrido in a small town in California? How could Tanya Nicole Kach be held in the bedroom of her school security guard in his parents' home in a suburb of Pennsylvania for ten years without anyone noticing? And how could Colleen Stan be kept in a box under the bed of a couple in Red Bluff, California, who only brought her out to humiliate, torture and rape her?

Back in the 1980s, Gary Heidnik established a basement baby farm in his home in Philadelphia where he beat, tortured and raped six women, one of whom he tortured to death. Then there was John Jamelske who held five women as sex slaves, one after another, over 15 years before he was caught.

The world was equally shocked when Elisabeth Fritzl emerged from the cellar of the family home in Austria after 24 years and having given birth to eight children sired by her own father. This came less than two years after another Austrian girl named Natascha Kampusch emerged after 3,096 days in captivity in a cellar. It was followed by the case of what the newspapers dubbed 'the British Fritzl', who kept his daughters isolated by moving frequently while fathering seven children by them.

In Belgium, two young girls were found in the cellar of convicted child molester Marc Dutroux, sparking a political scandal that reached the highest levels of society. Even in Russia, a former army officer put two girls in a cellar to rape them and impregnate them.

But those who disappear from the streets are not only held for sex. While the Cleveland case was unravelling, it was discovered that four men were being held in Houston for their social security cheques. In Britain, a handful of men were held for up to 15 years by a family who forced them to work while holding them in the most squalid conditions.

But this book is not about the monsters who thrive on the

misery of others. *The Disappeared* is about the bravery of the survivors – particularly the women – who endured the unendurable and came out fighting. Often, they have simply outsmarted their captors who somehow imagined that they were intellectually superior to their victims. While the perpetrators demonstrate the extreme depths of depravity to which human beings can sink, the survivors show the heights of courage attainable by the human spirit.

Al Cimino
Bloomsbury, 2014

PART 1

THE CLEVELAND KIDNAPPINGS

1

ESCAPE
FROM HELL

On Monday, 6 May 2013, Ariel Castro left his house at 2207 Seymour Avenue, Cleveland, Ohio. It was a three-storey clapboard building with a detached garage, standing in the middle of a tree-lined street in Cleveland's West Side neighbourhood – a working-class area with a close-knit community. Ariel Castro had bought the four-bedroom house from Edwin and Antonia Castro in 1992 for $12,000 (£7,750). It was now valued at $36,100 (£23,300), but faced repossession over the non-payment of taxes. Castro owed some $2,501 (£1,615) in taxes for the period 2010–12. The property had four bedrooms, a bathroom, a 760sq ft (71sq m) basement, two porches and an attic. It is just steps away from a petrol station and a Caribbean grocery. Other than being a bit run down, there was nothing at all extraordinary about it – except that it held a terrible secret.

Ariel Castro's son Anthony had visited the house just two

weeks before and noticed that the doors to the basement, the attic and the garage were padlocked. He had spent his early years in this house, but most of the rooms were off limits even to family members. Ariel Castro's ex-wife, Grimilda 'Nilda' Figueroa, Anthony and his three sisters moved out of the house in 1996 after years of violent abuse. Since then, Anthony seldom visited.

'The house was always locked,' recalled Anthony. 'There were places we could never go. There were locks on the basement ... locks on the attic ... locks on the garage.'

In fact, on that visit Anthony had not even been invited inside. Visits, when he made them, were brief. 'I haven't been at that house for longer than 20 minutes for longer than I can remember,' he said. 'And we're talking since high school. Late nineties.'

To the neighbours, Ariel Castro, a school bus driver, was just 'a regular Joe' who chatted with other families on their porches, waved hello in the street and invited neighbours to clubs where he played bass with several Latin bands. 'He was not a troublemaker,' said 58-year-old Jovita Marti, whose mother lived across the street.

Mike Kazimore, a local postman who delivered mail to the porch virtually every day for the previous 12 years, said, 'It looked like a normal house.'

Niki Greiner, another resident, said the property was usually quiet, although sometimes you would hear music. This broke the background hum of traffic, but was rarely loud enough to obscure the birdsong.

Some of the houses in the street had seen better days. The recession had taken its toll and paint peeled from a fair few of the one- and two-storey houses. As in many of the poorer areas

3

of American cities, a number of houses had been boarded up since the sub-prime mortgage crash. But it was not the kind of area where you felt menace on the streets. The people were friendly and happy to talk; residents like to sit out on their porches in the warm weather and watch the world go by, and the red-brick Immanuel Evangelical Lutheran Church with a large silver cross on the wall was well attended.

Ariel Castro had left home to visit his mother's house nearby that afternoon. He arrived at around 4.30pm. Other members of the family were there and he greeted them warmly. 'The first thing he said was, *"Familia!"*' said his 63-year-old brother-in-law, Juan Alicea.

After a meal of rice and beans and pork chops, Castro and Alicea did some digging in the garden with Alicea's two grandchildren. 'He was talking about how he wanted to get it done because he didn't want to have to come back and do it tomorrow,' said Alicea. 'Then he kissed his mom goodbye and said, "I love you, Mom. The food was good." Just like normal.'

But that day was not like normal. When he left the house, Castro had forgotten to lock the front door. Inside was 27-year-old Amanda Berry, one of three who had been held as a slave there for over a decade. All that stood between her and freedom was a flimsy storm door, but she was afraid to break it open because she thought that Castro might be testing her. Castro used a sick game to intimidate his captives; he would pretend to leave the door unlocked and beat them if they tried to escape.

This time, though, she plucked up all her courage and started screaming. Her cries alerted a neighbour, restaurant pot-washer Charles Ramsey, who was eating a hamburger.

He had spoken to Castro early that day. It was at around 3.00pm when Ramsey handed Castro his mail, which had been put in the wrong mailbox. He had seen Castro leave the house. Then Ramsey had got on his bike and cycled around to the local McDonald's. After he got back, he was in the living room by the front door when he heard Amanda's cries for help.

'Man, this girl screamed like a car had hit a kid, which made me, you know, stop eating. What the hell was that?' said Ramsey. 'You know, so when I got up, I saw this – my neighbour across the street, he run across the street and I'm like ... I'm thinking, where you going, because ain't nobody next door because I just saw Ariel leave.'

Curious, he went to investigate. His neighbour Angel Cordero was already outside Castro's house. But Cordero did not speak English very well so Ramsey went over to help out. Carrying his half-eaten Big Mac, Ramsey climbed up on to the porch and saw a girl inside. By then, Amanda was frightened and desperate.

'Help me get out,' she said. 'I've been in here a long time.'

'So, I'm like, "What's your problem? If you're stuck, just open the door,"' Ramsey remembers.

She said, 'I can't, you got it locked.'

They tried to prise the door open, but it would only open far enough for a hand to fit through.

'Lucky that door was aluminium,' said Ramsey. 'It was cheap.'

So he and Cordero kicked in the bottom panel and Amanda crawled out carrying her six-year-old daughter, Jocelyn. It had been Jocelyn who had prompted the escape attempt. She had told her mother, 'Daddy's gone to see Grandma.' That meant he would be away for some time.

'Bro, I knew something was wrong when a pretty little white girl ran into a black man's arms,' said Ramsey. 'Something's wrong here. Dead giveaway, dead giveaway! Dead giveaway, because either she's homeless or she's got problems, because that's the only reason she run to a black man.'

Later, he told a TV interviewer, 'Let me tell you something. I'm American, and I'm a human being. I'm just like you. There was a woman in distress, so why turn your back on that? My father would have whupped the hell out of me if he had found out that I cowered out. I'm the definition of a man, bro.'

Within hours, the interview had become an Internet sensation. Charles had his own Twitter hashtag – #Chuck Ramsay. A video remix of his 'pretty little white girl' comment had been released, and he even secured a manager.

Neighbour Angie Garcia was also on hand. 'The screen door had glass at the bottom with wood,' she said. 'My friend helped break down the door. She had half her body out. The little girl kept saying, "Mommy! Mommy!"'

Amanda appeared nervous, crying and was dressed in pyjamas and old sandals, according to one description. Once free she said, 'Call 911 ... my name is Amanda Berry.'

'When she told me, it didn't register,' said Ramsey.

But Cordero recognized Amanda from the missing-persons posters that appeared regularly round the area. He did not speak English, though. He said that Amanda appeared ragged. Her clothes were dirty, her teeth were yellow and her hair was messy, and that the child with her had looked very nervous, as though she had never seen anything outside the house before.

Ramsey told a different story; he said Amanda was wearing a jumpsuit. 'She had a white tank-top on, rings on, mascara,' he said. 'You know, she was well groomed. She didn't look like she was kidnapped. That's what I'm saying. That's what threw me off. She was like, "I'm in here trapped." I'm like, well, you don't look kidnapped so maybe you got a boyfriend problem. But I'm thinking I know who lives here and he's 50-something. You can't be the boyfriend problem. You know? It can't be him. Maybe you're dating his son.'

While Ramsey had never seen Amanda before, he had heard kids playing in the back garden which he figured were Castro's grandchildren. Nevertheless, Ramsey did what he was told and called 911. He told the dispatcher with typical bluntness, 'This broad is trying to break out of the fucking house next to me!'

'You have to calm down and slow down,' replied dispatcher.

'I'm looking at her right now,' Ramsey said. 'She's calling y'all. She's on another phone.'

'Sir, we can't talk at the same time,' said the dispatcher. 'Do you want to leave your name and number?' After some back and forth, the dispatcher asked Ramsey if the woman needed an ambulance.

'She needs everything. She's in a panic, bro. I guess she's just been kidnapped. Put yourself in her shoes.'

While Cordero held the child, Amanda had called 911 on a phone belonging to another neighbour named Anna Tejeda.

'Help me, I'm Amanda Berry,' Amanda told the operator.

'Do you need police, fire or ambulance?' came the reply.

'I need police,' said Amanda.

'OK, and what's going on there?' said the operator.

'I've been kidnapped and I've been missing for ten years and I'm here. I'm free now,' said Amanda, choking back the tears.

'OK, and what's your address?' said the operator while trying to figure out where Amanda was.

'2207 Seymour Avenue.'

'2207 Seymour? Looks like you are calling me from 2210,' the operator replied.

'Huh?' said Amanda, puzzled.

'It looks like you are calling me from 2210.'

'I'm across the street. I'm using their phone,' said Amanda.

'OK, stay there with those neighbours and talk to the police when they get there.'

'OK,' said Amanda, sobbing.

'Talk to the police when they get there,' the operator repeated.

'OK. Hello?' said Amanda, who was losing her grip on the situation.

'Yeah, talk to the police when they get there.'

'OK, I don't want to leave right now.' There was a pause. 'OK, are they on their way right now?' asked Amanda. 'I need them now.'

The operator said that a car would be sent as soon as one was available. 'We're gonna send them as soon as we get a car open.'

'No, I need them now before he gets back,' said Amanda.

'All right,' said the operator. 'We're sending them, OK?'

Amanda became frantic. 'OK. I mean, like, right now,' she insisted. 'I need them now before he gets back.'

'Who is the guy who went out?' asked the operator.

'His name is Ariel Castro,' said Amanda.

'All right. How old is he?'

'He's, like, 52.'

'All right, and a ...'

By this time Amanda was becoming increasingly frustrated. 'And I'm Amanda Berry. I've been on the news for the last ten years.'

Plainly, this meant nothing to the 911 operator. 'OK, I got that, dear,' she said. 'What is his name again?'

'Uh, Ariel Castro,' said Amanda.

'And is he white, black or Hispanic?'

'Uh, he's Hispanic.'

The operator then asked Amanda what her captor had been wearing.

'I don't know 'cause he's not here right now,' replied Amanda, sobbing again. 'That's how we got away.'

'When he left, what was he wearing?'

It is impossible to make out her reply, but the operator reassured her. 'The police are on the way,' she said. 'Talk to them when they get there.'

It was only when Ramsey overheard Amanda's call that he realized who she was. 'It didn't register until I got the call to 911 and I thought, "I'm calling 911 for Amanda Berry? I thought this girl was dead,"' he said.

Anna Tejeda could not believe her ears either. 'You're not Amanda Berry,' she insisted. 'Amanda Berry is dead.'

Ramsey could not believe that Ariel Castro was

responsible either. It was over a year since Ramsey had moved into the area and he had got to know his neighbour pretty well and had never suspected that anything was amiss. 'I barbecued with this dude,' said Ramsey. 'We eat ribs and whatnot and listen to salsa music. I had no clue that that girl was in that house or anybody else was in there against their will, because of how he is. He just comes out to his backyard, plays with the dogs, tinkers with his cars and motorcycles, goes back in the house. He's somebody who you look at and then you look away because he's just doing normal stuff. There's nothing exciting about him. Well, until today... You got to have some big testicles to pull this one off because we see this guy every day,' he added.

Ramsey was about to enter Castro's house when the police arrived. Officer Anthony Espada was one of the first on the scene. He had already been alerted that the caller had identified herself as the long-sought-after Amanda Berry.

Driving up to the house, Espada saw a crowd on the porch with a girl. She was holding a child and raised her hand. Espada then turned to his partner and said, 'Is it her?'

He said, 'I can't tell.'

'We were pulling up closer,' said Espada, 'and as soon as we pull up, my partner was driving, so she came up to the driver's side. He looked up at me and he's like, "It is her."'

The relief of the rescue was quickly put aside when the officers weighed the possibility that Berry's captor was inside the house. 'We figured he might possibly be in the house because she kept pointing at the house,' said Espada.

His partner then asked her if anyone was still inside.

To their surprise, Amanda replied, 'Yes. Gina DeJesus and another girl.'

'It was like another bombshell with overwhelming force just hit me,' said Espada.

Amanda told them that the girls were being held upstairs, not in the basement. The officers then crawled into the house through the hole in the broken storm door. Inside, they said the conditions were 'abysmal at best'. With guns drawn, they made their way upstairs. On the landing, the officers called out saying that they were the Cleveland Police. Then one of the officers saw a pair of eyes peeking through a slightly opened bedroom door. The eyes belonged to 32-year-old Michelle Knight.

'She kinda popped out into the doorway and paused there for a second,' said Espada. 'I mean, within moments she came charging at me. She jumped on to me. She's like, "You saved us! You saved us!"'

Then 23-year-old Gina DeJesus appeared from a bedroom.

'I just look at her,' Espada recalled. 'You can immediately tell who it is.'

He asked her, 'What's your name?'

'My name is Georgina DeJesus,' she replied.

The officers could hardly believe that they had solved three missing-persons cases in one go. Espada quickly radioed in, 'We found them! We found them!'

Despite the presence of the police, the three women were plainly terrified and in a rundown state. 'They were very dirty. Real bad-looking,' said neighbour Angie Garcia. 'They hadn't showered ... their teeth were yellow.'

Then, as police and neighbours converged on the house, Castro was seen coming around the corner.

'As soon as he saw the police, he turned and left,' said Garcia. But, at the time, the police were more concerned about the victims.

After the dramatic rescue, FBI Special Agent Steve Anthony said, 'The nightmare is over. These three young ladies have provided us with the ultimate definition of survival and perseverance. Words can't describe the emotions being felt by all.' He added, 'Yes, law enforcement professionals do cry.'

According to Amanda Berry, it was not the first time that Castro had forgotten to lock the front door. In his haste to get something to eat, he sometimes only locked a screen door. Usually, he would only be away a short time. And normally they would not be allowed to roam around the house. Ropes, chains and padlocks were found on the premises.

A creature of habit, Castro was arrested in a McDonald's nearby.

2

MICHELLE KNIGHT

Michelle Knight was 21 when she disappeared on 23 August 2002 – the year the USA and its allies invaded Afghanistan. She was last seen at a cousin's house. Family members, police and social workers all concluded that she had run away of her own accord, angry that her son Joey had been taken from her by the Ohio Department of Family Services.

But her mother, Barbara, was unable to accept that Michelle would vanish without a word. She was sure that her daughter would at least call her to let her know she was safe. Barbara continued distributing flyers in Cleveland long after police had stopped searching. Even when she moved to Florida, she would often return to Cleveland to continue her search.

Once she thought she saw Michelle walking through a shopping plaza in the city. She was walking with an older man, who appeared to be dragging her along when she dawdled. But when Barbara called her daughter's name, the woman did not turn round.

Her mother said that Michelle had spent most of her life on Cleveland's West Side, with many of the happiest days of her childhood spent in a house on West 60th Street, where she helped her mother work in her vegetable garden. By the time she disappeared, the family had moved to Walton Avenue.

As a child, Michelle became fascinated by the fire engines that would race down their street on their way to emergencies. After a tour of the local fire station, she set her heart on becoming a firefighter herself one day.

Michelle loved animals, too. She loved to feed apples to the neighbour's pet pony and, after she helped her mother deliver the family shih tzu's litter of puppies, she decided to become a vet instead. She loved school, especially art, where she developed a talent for sketching. She had a lot of good friends there.

Family members say Knight was just a regular, everyday kid who loved music, especially the songs of Christina Aguilera. 'I used to babysit her,' said her aunt, Nellie White. 'When she found out I was pregnant with Tiffani, she was so excited. She was a really bright girl. She was not out of control. She was the best kid ever.'

Michelle's troubles began when she was 17 when she was the victim of bullying. Then she claimed she had been sexually assaulted by two boys in the school lavatories. They pulled her into the toilet and raped her, said her grand-mother, Deborah White. She reported the incident to police, but felt that her story was not taken seriously.

Soon afterward, Michelle fell pregnant and dropped out

of school. After she gave birth, though, she dreamed of completing her education so she could provide a better life for her son. 'She recovered and took care of the baby with her mom's help,' said her grandmother.

However, Barbara Knight then started a new relationship. Sometime after this Michelle lost custody of her son. A custody hearing was scheduled for the day she went missing. Her grandmother, who lived not far from Seymour Avenue, said, 'After that we never saw her again ... we tried to get the baby. He is out there someplace, and we have no idea where he is.'

The Cleveland Police's missing-person report detailing Michelle Knight's disappearance said that she had a mental condition and often was confused by her surroundings. It said she was last seen at a cousin's house near West 106th Street and Lorain Avenue, and noted that she was nick-named 'Shorty' as she was only 4ft 7in tall.

The case went nowhere because Michelle was already 20 years old at the time of her disappearance and the police were not 100 per cent sure she had been abducted. Even her grandmother Deborah thought Michelle may have run away because she was upset over losing custody of her son. 'We thought she might have been with friends she knew,' Deborah said.

After filing the report, Barbara Knight said the police did little to investigate the disappearance, believing that Michelle probably left of her own accord, embittered by the custody battle. But Barbara insisted that running away was not in her daughter's nature. She told Cleveland's *Plain Dealer* that she never believed her daughter would run away and kept searching for Michelle.

'I know she was an adult at the time,' said Barbara's stepson Frank, 'but the Cleveland Police, they lack a lot.'

Barbara papered Cleveland's West Side with flyers and, even after moving out of the state, would often return to continue the search on her own. She was frequently frustrated by the lack of help she got from the city's police. She had given them a photograph of her daughter when she filed the missing-persons report, but was disheartened when it did not appear alongside those of Amanda Berry and Gina DeJesus when they, too, went missing. As a result, she had no other photo of Michelle to provide to the media, who took little interest in her disappearance.

Unlike the other two girls, Michelle was an adult when she disappeared. There was no mention of Michelle on any missing-persons websites; neither the FBI websites nor the Ohio Attorney General's website carried her details.

It was reported in the Cleveland *Plain Dealer* that the Cleveland Police had removed Michelle Knight's missing-persons entry from the FBI database 15 months after she disappeared because they could not reach her mother on the telephone in November 2003 to confirm that she was still missing. However, the police department's written policy on investigating missing adults describes a different verification process. It states that a missing person is only removed from the National Crime Information Center database after an officer has gone to see the person who has been found. Then they must inform the FBI within two hours.

Kym Pasqualini, founder of the National Center for Missing Adults, which has helped track down thousands of missing persons, said that the removal of Michelle's name and description from the database helped the case fall through the cracks. The NCIC database, which the FBI refers to as 'the lifeline of law enforcement', is an electronic clearing house of crime data. When a missing person's information is entered, it becomes available to law enforcement agencies nationwide. Michelle's family would have needed an NCIC number if they sought assistance from Pasqualini's organization or any other non-profit agency that deals with missing-person cases.

Pasqualini acknowledged that the inclusion of Amanda Berry and Gina DeJesus on the NCIC database did not help law enforcement officials locate them sooner. However, invalidation of Michelle Knight's case indicated a larger systemic problem – that missing juveniles are a higher priority than missing adults. 'If a missing person is in the NCIC system, it instantly legitimizes the case,' Pasqualini said. 'Had Michelle's mother called us for help, we would have had to say no.'

While Michelle Knight had been removed from the FBI database, her police file shows that officers continued to enquire about her whereabouts for years afterwards. Entries show that officers tried to reach Knight's mother by phone and, through May 2003, successfully verified that Knight was still missing. But on 13 November 2003, a detective tried again to contact Michelle's mother on a landline and left a message. 'No new info available at this time,' the detective wrote. 'This report will remain invalid until new leads develop.'

Half a dozen similar notes appear throughout the rest of the file. In one instance, an officer attempted to reach the missing woman herself by calling her mobile phone. 'I tried to reach Michelle Knight ... with negative results,' the officer's report dated 1 December 2004 said.

Until the discovery of the three woman on 6 May 2013, the DeJesus and Berry cases were still featured in Cleveland Police's own online missing-person database, among the very oldest of more than a hundred unsolved cases. Michelle Knight's was not. But her mother had to sit and watch the publicity surrounding the search for Amanda Berry and Gina DeJesus while her daughter barely got a mention.

Judy Martin, founder of the Cleveland advocacy group Survivors/Victims of Tragedy, also said that Michelle Knight's case had simply 'slipped through the cracks'. Active in the hunt for Amanda Berry and Gina DeJesus, Martin said, 'If it hadn't been for the families in these two cases, nothing would have been done.'

But her mother had not given up hope. 'I really miss her,' Barbara Knight told *The Plain Dealer*. 'She was my daughter, but she was also my friend. She tried to make the best of her life and wanted to finish school. She never got the chance to go back.'

On the night she went missing, Michelle had foolishly accepted a lift from Castro who lured her to his Seymour Avenue home with the promise of a present for her son. She found herself chained in the basement where she was beaten, raped and starved. After a year, she was eventually allowed to live unchained upstairs. She was kept behind locked doors with holes cut in them so Castro could slide food in. Like the others, she was fed a constant diet of fast food. As a result, their teeth were yellow and they were malnourished.

After the other girls were kidnapped, Michelle knew they were in the house, but she was allowed little contact with them. Each year on 23 August, she would be given cake to celebrate her 'abduction day', a cruel ritual Castro repeated with his other captives. Occasionally, they were allowed out in the garden, but had to wear wigs and sunglasses, and keep their heads down.

During her captivity, Michelle fell pregnant five times, but Castro would punch her in the stomach to induce a miscarriage. His regular beatings also resulted in hearing loss. Castro also forced Michelle to deliver Amanda Berry's baby and threatened to kill her if the child died. The baby girl stopped breathing at one point and Michelle had to give her mouth-to-mouth resuscitation.

While Barbara Knight had never bought the story that her daughter had run away and kept searching for her tirelessly over the years, she did not believe the first stories about her daughter being found. Despite her doubts, she said, 'I'm praying that if it is her, she will come back with me, so I can help her recover from what she has been through. So much has happened in these ten years. She has a younger sister she still has not met.'

After it was confirmed that Michelle had been found, Cleveland's Deputy Police Chief Ed Tomba acknowledged that, while an effort had been made to find Amanda Berry and Gina DeJesus over the last decade, Michelle Knight 'was the focus of very few tips'. He promised the whole of Michelle Knight's story would now come out.

3

AMANDA BERRY

On 16 April 2003, eight months after Michelle Knight went missing and soon after the beginning of the Iraq War, 16-year-old Amanda Berry called her older sister Beth to say that she was getting a lift home from the Burger King restaurant on West 110th Street and Lorain Avenue on Cleveland's West Side where she had a part-time job. It was the day before her 17th birthday and the two of them had spent most of the day making plans for her birthday party. Amanda finished work at around 7.30pm and the lift was to have taken her just three blocks.

'I've got a ride,' she said. 'I'll call you back.'

She never did, and she never arrived home. It would be ten years before she saw her family again.

When Amanda did not arrive home from work at her normal time, her mother Louwana Miller assumed something had upset her and she'd gone to a friend's house to calm down. But early the next morning, when Amanda still had not returned home, her mother called the police and reported her missing.

A happy teenager, remembered for a beaming smile, she would never see her mother again. Louwana Miller died in 2006, three years after the disappearance of her daughter. Friends said she had not been able to bear the anguish any longer. It took a toll on her health, which steadily deteriorated. 'She literally died of a broken heart,' said Dona Brady, a local councillor and friend of the family.

Louwana comforted herself with the idea that her daughter's last words to her were, 'Goodbye, Mom ... I love you.'

A year before she died, Louwana got her chance to put Amanda's photograph in front of the eyes of millions of Americans on *The Montel Williams Show*. Also appearing was television psychic Sylvia Browne.

'Can you tell me ... is she out there?' Louwana Miller asked.

'I hate when they're in the water,' Browne said. 'She's not alive, honey. Your daughter's not the kind who wouldn't call.'

This was the last thing that Louwana wanted to hear. 'So you don't think I'll ever see her again?' she said.

'Yeah, in heaven on the other side,' Browne responded. 'I'm sorry.'

Montel Williams then took a commercial break and Louwana broke down. Amanda's mother had faith in psychics. 'It hurts my mind but it eases it, now I know,' she said. 'I can't understand why, she was such a good girl. She didn't bother anybody.'

Many people were disturbed that Browne should deliver such a devastating conclusion based on her psychic insight.

'Are you ever wrong?' Browne was asked.

'Only God is right all the time but of course I'm wrong,' she replied. 'But after fifty years of doing this work, I'd better be more right than wrong. I always say I hope I'm wrong. When it comes to this, I hope I'm wrong.'

Nevertheless, the psychic was confident enough to offer more thoughts, this time concerning a suspect. 'I think he really had a crush on her,' she said. 'And I think she rebuffed him. I think she thought he was harmless enough to maybe drive her home.' She even envisioned Amanda's jacket in a dumpster with 'DNA on it'.

Despite the psychic's inaccurate comments, Louwana Miller hoped the show would prompt viewers to call in with useful clues. It didn't. Instead, she said she believed the psychic '98 per cent'. She went back to her West Side home in Cleveland where, until then, she had been keeping Amanda's things as she had left them. She gave away her daughter's computer, took down her pictures and cleared away her daughter's possessions. For years, Louwana had kept Amanda's room exactly as it was, said Tina Miller, a cousin. When magazines addressed to Amanda arrived, they were kept alongside the presents Louwana had bought for birthdays and Christmases Amanda had missed.

'I'm not even buying my baby a Christmas present this year,' said Louwana afterwards. Until Sylvia Browne dropped her bombshell, Louwana had been holding out hope that her daughter was still alive. 'Please don't misunderstand me. I still don't want to believe it,' she told a newspaper. 'I want to have hope but, after a year-and-a-half, what else is there? It seems like the God-honest truth. My daughter would always call home.' Even so, the following month, Amanda's family and friends convened for a prayer vigil at the corner of West 110th and Lorain near where she had disappeared.

The FBI and police said they would still assume that Amanda Berry was alive and missing until her body was discovered or evidence was found to prove otherwise. But, by then, the police had exhausted the very few leads they had to follow. They had tried to retrace the missing girl's steps, but they had found nothing that gave them any clues. She was last seen walking northwards on West 110th Street.

The driver who had offered to take her home was never identified and the police put out an appeal for anyone who had seen the pair in a car. A tip-off was reported to the police that Amanda had been seen getting into a white sedan with three men, but the source was not considered reliable, and the facts were never substantiated.

The police circulated a description of Amanda: she was 5ft 1in tall, weighed less than 8st and had long, sandy-blonde hair; her eyes were brown; she had piercings in her ears and an eyebrow, and a scar across her stomach from surgery she had had as a child. When she went missing, she was carrying a small black shoulder bag, in which she kept her silver mobile phone, along with a pack of Newport cigarettes, her regular brand. When she disappeared, she was still wearing her Burger King uniform.

It was clear that she had not run off. She had left $100 in her bedroom that she planned to spend on a new dress and a manicure for her birthday party.

'I don't understand where I stand,' her mother told a local

newspaper the following month. 'I don't know if she's out there being held ... I don't know if she's out there laying on the side of the road somewhere. Who gave her that ride?'

Her mother could not eat or sleep, and chain-smoked Marlboro cigarettes. Then, seven months later, there was a lead. Someone used Amanda's cell phone to call her mother. A man's voice said, 'I have Amanda. She's fine and will be coming home in a couple of days.'

The caller appeared to be between 18 and 30 years of age, Louwana said. He called again soon after, saying that he was married to her daughter. But when Louwana asked to speak to Amanda, he hung up. At first, she feared this was a prank as the call came on the same day her daughter's picture had appeared on television, but the FBI confirmed that the call had come from her daughter's mobile phone.

'This leads us to believe she was not a runaway,' said FBI agent Robert Hawk. 'Someone had control of her cell phone.'

But neither the call nor the phone could be traced. Once more, the trail went cold, although the FBI offered a reward of up to $25,000 for information leading to her return.

Louwana Miller was never the same after the television psychic's message. A friend at the time said, 'I think she had given up hope.' She was just 44 when she died of heart failure.

The following year, aged 20, Amanda Berry gave birth to a daughter, fathered by Ariel Castro, the man who had abducted and raped her. She had the baby in a child's inflatable paddling pool Castro had bought 'so the mess would be easier to clean up'. Her daughter, Jocelyn, was delivered by Michelle Knight, whose only previous experience was delivering her family's shih tzu's litter of puppies. With the thin wooden walls of the houses in Seymour Avenue, which sit only feet apart, it is surprising that neighbours did not hear the sounds of childbirth.

The girls did their best to educate the child, but she was never told their real names. Castro would sometimes take Jocelyn out, and he did not want to risk her repeating them in public.

Throughout Amanda's long captivity, the police continued their investigation. After the fourth anniversary of Amanda's disappearance, they circulated an age-progressed photograph showing what Amanda might look like at the age of 21. A tip-off led them to a girl who looked almost exactly like Amanda, but it turned out to be a case of mistaken identity.

In 2009, the Fond du Lac County Sheriff's Office in Wisconsin believed a frozen corpse found by deer hunters had similarities to Amanda, but a DNA test proved it was not the missing girl. Another 'Jane Doe' body found in California was thought to be Amanda but, again, this turned out to be a dead end.

Then, in 2012, a man telephoned the authorities, saying that he knew where to find Amanda's body. The tip-off came from prison inmate Robert Wolford who was serving 26 years for murder. It was not the news the family were hoping for, but at least they might be able to give her a proper burial, grieve for her and bring a close to this traumatic, ongoing heartache.

Wolford was taken to the location at the corner of Wade and West 30th Street, near Interstate 90, just two blocks from Seymour Avenue. He also said that another person was involved in the teenager's disappearance, but declined to give the person's name, although he said there was an outstanding warrant for his arrest.

The empty lot was dug up, but no body was found. Wolford was subsequently sentenced to four-and-a-half years in jail for obstructing justice and making a false report after admitting his story was a hoax.

Chillingly, Castro's elder brother Pedro looked on while the forensic team moved in. Sitting on the stoop of a house, wearing a floral shirt and sunglasses, Castro gestured to the lot and told reporters that looking for Amanda Berry's body was 'a waste of money'. He also warned neighbours that the police were wasting their time if they were looking for Gina's body.

'He told us they aren't going to find the bones in there,' said a neighbour. 'Now we know why – his brother had them in that house.'

When she crawled out of the storm door of Castro's house, Amanda Berry found she had not been forgotten. 'She was my best friend,' said her 26-year-old cousin Tasheena Mitchell.

'She *is* your best friend,' onlookers quickly corrected her.

The discovery that Amanda Berry was still alive prompted a backlash on Sylvia Browne's Facebook page. 'You told her mother that you saw her dead and laying in water almost ten years ago! Guess what, she's alive! Guess you were wrong! You put her mother through hell!!' said one.

'I remember you on *Montel Williams* telling the family of Amanda Berry she was dead ... What do you have to say for yourself? What a horrible, horrible thing to say to a family holding on to nothing but hope and faith ... Shame on you!' another said.

It was not the first time Browne had been wrong about a missing child. Four months after 11-year-old Shawn Hornbeck went missing while riding his bicycle near his home in Richmond, Missouri in 2002, Browne told his parents, again on *The Montel Williams Show*, that Shawn was dead and buried near some jagged boulders within 20 miles of their home. Four years later, he was found with another kidnapped child in the apartment of paedophile Michael J Devlin in Kirkwood, Missouri, 200 miles away.

Browne refused to speak with CNN host Anderson Cooper after the boy was found alive, but her spokesperson released this statement: 'She cannot possibly be 100 per cent correct in each and every one of her predictions. She has, during a career of over fifty years, helped literally tens of thousands of people.'

When Amanda Berry was also found alive, Browne made a similarly robust defence. She issued a statement saying, 'For more than fifty years as a spiritual psychic and guide, when called upon to either help authorities with missing-person cases or to help families with questions about their loved ones, I have been more right than wrong. If ever there was a time to be grateful and relieved for being mistaken, this is that time. Only God is right all the time. My heart goes out to Amanda Berry, her family, the other victims and their families. I wish you a peaceful recovery.'

Her representatives also forwarded a statement from Amanda's cousin Sherry Cole to the media. It said, 'Our family in no way blames Sylvia. This doesn't change any-thing. We still love her and believe in her.'

THE DISAPPEARED

But CNN's Anderson Cooper was less forgiving: 'In 2004, self-proclaimed "psychic" Sylvia Browne told Amanda Berry's mother her daughter was dead. Has she no shame?'

4

GINA
DEJESUS

Georgina 'Gina' DeJesus was just 14 when she disappeared after heading home from Wilbur Wright Middle School on the chilly afternoon of 2 April 2004, the year of the Athens Olympics. She was last seen around West 110th Street and Lorain Avenue, just blocks away from where Amanda had vanished. No concrete evidence linked the two cases, although there were many similarities. Both girls were young, attractive teenagers; they were both heading home on the same street as it began to get dark; both girls disappeared without anyone seeing anything; and both cases yielded surprisingly few promising leads.

'When I came home and I got on the phone from 4.00pm, I started calling friends and they said they did not see her,' said Gina's mother Nancy Ruiz.

'She would never run away,' her aunt, Peggy Arida, said.

But when the family contacted the police, no AMBER

Alert was issued because no one witnessed her abduction. The 'America's Missing: Broadcast Emergency Response' alert system had been introduced after nine-year-old Amber Hagerman was abducted in Arlington, Texas, in 1996. It issues alerts through all electronic media when a child goes missing. Amber had been found dead four days after her disappearance.

The lack of an AMBER Alert angered her father, Felix DeJesus, who said he believed the public would listen even if the alerts become routine. 'The AMBER Alert should work for any missing child,' Felix DeJesus said. 'It doesn't have to be an abduction. Whether it's an abduction or a runaway, a child needs to be found. We need to change this law.'

Cleveland Police responded, saying that the alerts must be reserved for cases where danger is imminent and the public may be of help in locating the suspect and the child. Again, the FBI offered a cash reward for her return.

At first, there was speculation that Gina had run away because she had recently been grounded for smoking. But as she did not return in the next few days, the authorities became convinced she had been abducted or murdered, and people were asked to look out for a girl with pierced ears and a birthmark on her right leg.

Four days after Gina disappeared, her mother Nancy marked her birthday without her daughter by her side. She put on a brave face, although she was finding it difficult to sleep, while Felix went to A&E with chest pains. Nevertheless, it was not long before he was putting up posters of his daughter on the West Side. Meanwhile, FBI technicians were going through security camera videotapes from four stores along Lorain and Clark Avenues. And 25 sheriff's deputies tracked down offenders living in Gina's neighbourhood who were wanted on warrants. Seven were arrested.

'We're just trying to shake some trees and see if we can get any information,' Chief Deputy Charles Corrao said. 'I'm personally tired of these animals taking our children.'

Police and city officials also attended a packed meeting in the auditorium of Gina's school. They implored parents to press their children for any information that could aid the investigation. 'We have followed up on every possible lead we have and we will continue to do so,' Mayor Jane Campbell told a crowd of nearly 500. 'We still do not have a grip on where Gina is. We have to have every bit of information.'

Frustration over the handling of the previous unsolved disappearances in the neighbourhood erupted with residents accusing Campbell of ignoring the earlier cases. Several angry residents had to be ushered out by the police.

At separate assemblies, children were instructed about how to stay safe in their neighbourhoods. Students were also asked for any information they might have about Gina and were given time to discuss possible leads with officers privately. 'The information to be gathered is of prime importance,' said Cleveland schools' Chief Executive Officer, Barbara Byrd-Bennett.

Police sent Gina's information to two national organizations that help find missing children. The National Center for Missing and Exploited Children posted Gina's photo on its website where she was listed as an 'endangered runaway'. Another group called 'A Child Is Missing' placed 2,700 calls to household phones within a half-mile radius of Gina's home to seek information on her disappearance.

There was no indication of violence surrounding Gina's

disappearance, police said. Gina had left the school on Parkhurst Drive at around 2.30pm that Friday. She and a friend walked to West 105th Street and Lorain Avenue, where they split up. Gina walked at least one more block down Lorain Avenue. After that, she disappeared.

The friend she had walked with was Arlene Castro, the daughter of her abductor and a classmate at school. She borrowed 50¢ to call her mother to ask if the two of them could hang out at Gina's for the rest of the afternoon. When her mother said no, they went their separate ways. 'Well, I'll talk to you later,' said Gina and walked off.

Later, police dogs tracked DeJesus's scent to the payphone Castro had used.

Normally, Gina would have taken the bus but, after she had given Arlene 50¢ for the phone call, she did not have enough money for the bus fare. So she headed home on foot. Tracker dogs followed her scent halfway down the next block. Then the trail went cold. A description was circulated; she was last seen wearing a tan shirt, light blue jacket and black pants.

Commander Gary Gingell, who was heading the investigation, said the police were treating her disappearance as a possible abduction and a runaway case. They were also examining a separate kidnapping and rape case to see if there were connections. A teenage girl said a man grabbed her as she waited for the bus near West 40th Street and Denison Avenue just ten days earlier. She told police the man had assaulted her, then let her go. The man in question was white, about 25 years old, 6ft tall and weighed about 14st. This led nowhere.

Rumours circulated that Gina's body had been found. Her

family told people to stop spreading these false rumours. 'We're hearing them daily,' Gina's cousin Sylvia Colon said. 'It's very difficult. Help us by not perpetuating those rumours. Stop spreading them, stop repeating them.'

The rumours persisted throughout Gina's captivity. Each time they were checked out and found to be unfounded.

Three months after DeJesus vanished, Ariel Castro's son and namesake who was studying journalism at Bowling Green State University wrote an article about the case for the local paper, the *Plain Press*. For it, he interviewed Gina's mother, Nancy Ruiz. The piece was headlined 'GINA DEJESUS' DISAPPEARANCE HAS CHANGED HER NEIGHBORHOOD' and Ruiz told him, 'You can tell the difference. People are watching out for each other's kids. It's a shame that a tragedy had to happen for me to really know my neighbours – bless their hearts, they've been great. People are really looking out for my daughter.'

There is no suggestion that Ariel Castro Jr knew that his father was involved. He later changed his name to Anthony and went into banking.

For the next nine years, Gina's family and friends held an annual vigil on the day she went missing. Among those who attended was her best friend Arlene Castro, whose father, unbeknown to her, was holding Gina.

Ruiz believed that her daughter had been a victim of human trafficking. 'I always said it from the beginning – she was sold to the highest bidder,' she said.

A year after Gina went missing, a sketch of her alleged abductor was released by the FBI and shown on the TV show *America's Most Wanted*. The FBI sketch shows a Hispanic man, between about 25 to 35 years old. He was described as being about 5ft 10in tall and weighing 165–185lb. He had a small beard and green eyes. Investigators said this was significant because green eyes are rare in the Hispanic community.

The day Gina went missing, two students noticed the man portrayed in the sketch in the vicinity but, at the time, investigators said they did not think it was significant. 'This didn't look like a good lead at the time,' said FBI agent Bob Hawk. 'It came in shortly after she was abducted. We didn't want people to lock into one person at that time. We had a lot of what we thought were really good leads. We covered those. They were unsuccessful.'

When the sketch was shown on *America's Most Wanted*, the FBI said they hoped someone would recognize the man and call in. Even then, investigators were not calling him a suspect. He was just a 'person of interest' they would like to talk to.

In fact, the sketch bore a striking resemblance to Ariel Castro. He was 5ft 10in and 178lb, with a small goatee. However, he was 43 at the time and had brown eyes.

While the sketch did not lead the FBI to Castro, they did interrogate Fernando Colon, the boyfriend of Castro's ex-wife Grimilda Figueroa. He was tailed by agents and forced to give a sample of DNA. Colon said that he told the FBI that Castro was a more likely suspect. However, Colon had been convicted of molesting two of Figueroa's daughters. That case, he claims, was driven by Castro, who testified against him in court. 'He's got these girls prisoner in there, and put an accusation as such to me, makes him look like an angel, like he is such a proud father, such a trustworthy person,' Colon told Fox8 television.

Chris Gianni, an investigator on Colon's defence team, said, 'They should have checked out his house and talked to him, and interviewed him, and thought about something.'

This time, it was Castro who fell through the cracks. 'Ariel wasn't investigated at all,' Frank Caraballo, Castro's former brother-in-law, said. 'Why was Arlene's actual father out of the picture? He's the bus driver, he knows where all these kids go.'

As Gina had disappeared almost a year after Amanda Berry, the police suspected that a serial attacker might be at work. In 2006, a tip-off led them to dig up a garage of a property belonging to a registered sex offender, but this again drew a blank. The house owner and another man living there were arrested on suspicion of aggravated murder. They were questioned, but a search of their home failed to yield anything, and neither man was charged.

In April 2009, the FBI said the cases of Amanda, Gina and Ashley Nicole Summers – who went missing in July 2007 – may have been the work of just one man as all three girls disappeared within five blocks of each other.

Ashley has yet to be found. The 14-year-old had been living with her great-uncle in the 2100 block of West 96th Street near Madison Avenue. She disappeared after an argument, taking all her clothes with her. She was 5ft 5in, weighed 130lb and had blue eyes and a tattoo on her right arm showing a heart with the name 'Gene' on it. And she was wearing a black shirt, blue jeans and white sneakers when she disappeared.

A month later, she called her mother to tell her not to worry, she was OK. Three months later, Ashley's step-grandmother thought she saw her on West 44th Street. Her brown hair had been cut short and dyed blonde. She was not heard of again.

Gina's family did not give up. Her mother would begin the search for her lost daughter all over again after each anniversary. Ariel Castro himself regularly turned out to help. He handed out flyers with the 14-year-old's picture on them and performed music at a fundraiser held in her honour. And, at the 2012 vigil, Castro was seen comforting the missing girl's mother.

'Ariel took part in the hunts for all three girls, but especially Amanda Berry and Gina DeJesus,' said Khalid Samad, former head of Cleveland Safety. 'We would put together a command centre and advertise it on TV and social media and he came along.'

His brothers Pedro and Onil would also take part in the searches. The trio would hand out flyers, while the kidnapped women were locked up just blocks away. 'Ariel acted his part very well,' said Samad. 'He had us all fooled. He acted like he was concerned and had empathy.'

Samad admitted that, even at the time, he had his suspicions. He saw Castro carrying bags of groceries and large orders, too much food for just one person.

Finally, thanks to the courage of Amanda Berry, the breakthrough came on 6 May, just before Mother's Day. Gina's cousin, 26-year-old Cecily Cruz, said she had heard about Gina's rescue from a customer at the gas station where she worked. She called her cousin's family immediately and said she could hear Gina's father in the background shouting, 'She's alive! They got my baby!'

Another cousin, Sylvia Colon, said, 'We were living every day in the hope she would come home – and she did.'

GINA DEJESUS

A third, Sheila Figaro, told CNN that the girl's mother, Nancy, 'never gave up faith, knowing that her daughter would one day be found. What a phenomenal Mother's Day gift she gets this Mother's Day.'

5

ARIEL
CASTRO

Ariel Castro was born in Puerto Rico. His father had run a used-car company in the city of Yauco, and was missing an arm after it had been chopped off with a machete during a gang dispute; he died in 2004. The family had emigrated to the USA – settling in Ohio – in the 1970s. His uncle, Julio 'Cesi' Castro, who was 78 when Ariel Castro was arrested, became a pillar of the Cleveland's Hispanic community, running the Carib Grocery Store on the corner of Seymour and West 25th Street at the end of Castro's block.

Ariel Castro was a school bus driver for 22 years before he was finally sacked in November 2012. The letter recommending his dismissal cited several transgressions by Castro – he had been suspended 60 days for leaving a child on a bus in January 2004; he was given another 60-day suspension for making an illegal U-turn in rush-hour traffic with a bus load of students in 2009; and again for using the school bus to do his grocery shopping in 2011. A charge of child abuse and neglect in 2004 were investigated by the Cuyahoga County Department of Children and Family Services. Officials called at Castro's house and got no answer; the charges were then found to be 'unsubstantiated'. He seems to have left a special-needs student locked in his bus while he went for lunch in Wendy's and told him to 'lay down, bitch', so that no one could see him.

The offence for which he was fired was leaving his bus unlocked and unattended at Scranton School. Castro claimed that his pre-school route was cancelled on that day and, because he lived only two blocks away, he went home. In a written response from an incident report, Castro said, 'Scranton is my school so I didn't think anything with parking there. I do apologize.'

In fact, there had been an earlier – violent – incident concerning the bus. In March 1993, two parents tried to board Castro's school bus, claiming that their son had been assaulted. The parents told police they had begun accompanying the boy to the bus stop in the morning. On that day, 'another such incident occurred in their presence,' the police report said. 'At which time, they got on the bus to stop it. However [they] were shoved by the driver,' the report claimed. Castro maintained that the parent shoved him back into his seat. No injuries were reported and the case was turned over to the Cleveland city schools. There was no record of any charges being preferred.

The police had to visit his home twice before. The first time was in 2000, before his first abduction, after Castro had reported a street fight. They also came to interview him in 2004 when two of his abductees were already there. When the police called, no one answered the door and they had no reason to make a forced entry, or procure a warrant.

Castro also had a history of domestic violence. He had been accused of assaulting his wife, Grimilda Figueroa, as well as menacing neighbours, at least six times as far back as 1989. Grimilda called the police and reported that Castro, her 'common-law husband of nine years', attacked her after she asked him where he was going with one of his brothers. After slapping her several times, 'he then grabbed her and slammed her several times against the wall and several times against the washing machine,' according to the report. She was treated at a hospital for a bruised right shoulder. She also told police she had been assaulted by Castro several other times, but had not reported the incidents. Figueroa was referred to the prosecutor's office, but there is no court record of any charge having been filed. The same year, Castro pleaded guilty to disorderly conduct.

In December 1993, he was arrested on domestic violence charges. Grimilda told police that Castro had thrown her to the ground and hit her about the head and kicked her body. It was a month after she had had brain surgery and she was prone to seizures. After the attack, their son fled through the front door; Castro chased him. Figueroa was then able to lock the door and Castro could not get back in. She called the police. When they arrived, Castro ran away and was chased by officers through a neighbour's yard and was arrested.

According to court documents, the mother of his children told the police that Castro had inflicted numerous injuries on her. The report said he had 'broken petitioner's nose (twice), ribs, lacerations, knocked out tooth, blood clot on brain, (inoperable tumour), dislocated shoulder, (twice, once on each side) threatened to kill petitioner and daughters three to four times just this year'.

Although Figueroa told police the next day she did not want to press charges, a city prosecutor filed charges of domestic violence and disorderly conduct. Castro pleaded guilty to disorderly conduct and a grand jury declined to indict him for domestic violence.

Her 75-year-old father, Ismail Figueroa, told the *New York Daily News* that once, when they lived upstairs in his home, Castro knocked his daughter down a staircase, leaving her with a broken arm and separated shoulder. When they moved out, Castro kept his wife isolated from her family. He locked her in the house – the same house where the three girls were kept captive – and refused to allow his kids outside the home, a grim foreshadowing of his future behaviour.

Another member of her family told ABC News that Castro was 'two-faced'; he was 'nice when he was outside but behind closed doors he was an animal,' she said, adding he had 'done terrible things' to her and treated her 'like trash'. The family blame Grimilda's early death on his relentless abuse.

The violence was not just directed against his wife. In November 1994, a man was checking on rental property near Castro's house and noticed his chain-link fence was missing. He went to Castro's home to enquire about it, and Castro became upset. Castro picked up a shovel and attempted to hit the man with it, then told him that 'he was going to take care of him'. The incident was referred to prosecutors, but there is no record of charges being filed.

In May 1996, a man whom relatives have described as

Figueroa's boyfriend after she left Castro was dropping his children off at school when Castro pulled up behind him and threatened him. When the man got out of his car to talk to him, Castro drove off. According to the police report, the man said, 'He believes that the named suspect would have run him over if he did not get out of his way.' Castro's behaviour was described as 'an ongoing problem' and was referred to prosecutors. But, again, there was no record of any charges being filed.

Three months later, a woman who described Castro as her ex-neighbour told the police he pulled in front of her driveway and screamed a threat before driving away. The police referred the woman to prosecutors. Yet again, there was no record of charges.

The most serious incident occurred when the police arrested Castro for abduction and child endangerment. This was over a 2004 incident where he left a child alone in the school bus while he went to a fast-food restaurant. It wasn't until about 2.00pm that he returned the child to his home, the report said. The child was then examined at Metro-Health Hospital and released. According to the report, Castro told police he noticed the boy in his seat and took the child home after consulting with the teacher by phone.

While the Cuyahoga County Department of Children and Family Services investigation found the charge of child abuse to be unsubstantiated, the police also investigated. The police also went to Castro's home to question him, but no one came to the door, City Safety Director Martin Flask said. They later interviewed Castro elsewhere, but they found that there was no criminal intent on Castro's part.

The domestic violence protection order was filed against

Castro on 29 August 2005. It alleged that, although Figueroa had full custody of their three children – Ariel (aka Anthony), Angie and Emily, Castro 'frequently abducts daughters and keeps them from mother/petitioner/legal custodian. Most recently threatened to kill her on 25 August 2005 and the children also.' The civil petition aimed to ensure Castro stayed away from Figueroa and her children for five years, but Figueroa never went through with the hearing.

Grimilda Figueroa had met her future husband when the Castros moved into the house opposite her family's home in the 1980s. Frank Caraballo, later Castro's brother-in-law, grew up next door to the house in Seymour Avenue and recalled going into the basement as a young boy. 'It's a little dungeon with one of those doors that you can lift up on the side,' he said. 'It's brick, old-fashioned, with one of those old trap doors.' This is where the women Castro abducted were initially held.

Grimilda's sister, Mrs Elida Caraballo, took against the Castro brothers from the beginning. 'I never did get along with them,' she said. 'I just never did.' She claimed that Ariel Castro frequently shoplifted and showed his fiery temper. 'He is a man with two faces,' she said. Nor was she surprised when Castro turned out to be a kidnapper and a rapist. 'Were we shocked by the news? The way Ariel was? No.'

But Castro's daughter Angie had suspected nothing; she had been at Castro's house hours before the captives emerged. 'She thought he was the perfect dad,' said Mrs Caraballo, who telephoned Angie at work to tell her that her father had been arrested. 'The next thing, she's saying to me,

"Wow, what a monster!"' Mrs Caraballo also detailed the violent ordeal of her sister. 'Everybody needs to know that my sister was abused by him,' she said. 'She was a victim. She didn't do anything but cook, clean and take care of her kids.'

Initially, they lived with their in-laws, which limited his opportunities to be violent. But when they moved into their own house, things got dramatically worse.

'All hell started breaking loose,' said Mrs Caraballo. 'I would go over to the house and be knocking at the door, and she was there and he wasn't, and I'd say, "Open the door," and she'd say, "I can't, he locked it." He broke her nose, her ribs, her arms. She was put into a box. He locked her in and told her, "When you're ready to come out, I'll tell you to come out."'

Frank Caraballo said that Castro had once beaten his wife so badly that he came to blows with his brother-in-law. 'I was hitting him, too, because I was tired of her being abused,' he said.

On one occasion, Castro sent his wife flying down a set of stairs, cracking her skull when she landed. She later blamed the fall for her brain tumour which eventually proved fatal.

Castro's behaviour worsened when the couple had children. His son, Anthony, described being beaten and banned from entering locked sections of the house. He was just as bad with the girls. 'He was so strict,' said Mr Caraballo. 'Angie was a little baby, and he wouldn't let us touch her. He didn't want anybody anywhere near his daughters.'

Castro's wife fled their home in Seymour Avenue after a particularly savage beating in 1996. After helping her remove her possessions, the police detained Castro, but again charges were not pressed.

Castro also suffered from road rage. According to Frank Carabello, he once provoked a furious dispute with a bodybuilder, who took a baseball bat from his car and smashed Castro's windscreen, showering the children with glass.

The Caraballos also said that their 19-year-old daughter, Elida-Marie, had visited Castro's house in recent years. 'She told us that the only thing he said was, "You stay in this room, and do not go in any other room. I want you to stay in this room only,"' said Mr Caraballo. 'She took it as him being rude. But she said he would always turn the radio up high. And before anybody could even visit, you'd have to wait 35–40 minutes before he would let you in.'

Grimilda Figueroa died in 2012, aged 48, following complications related to her brain tumour. Towards the end, 'she couldn't even stand up,' said Frank Caraballo. 'If she did, she would fall straight to the ground. And she was partially paralyzed. She blamed it all on Ariel.'

'There was so much severe pain,' her sister said.

Mrs Carabello also said that Castro and a brother turned up to her wake uninvited, drank heavily and cracked jokes.

Ariel's son Anthony, a 31-year-old banker living in Columbus, Ohio, when his father was arrested, said, 'I can express nothing but shame for our family that it involved any one of us. It's beyond comprehension. It's just beyond anything that anyone could really dream up. It's just a nightmare. I just feel unspeakably horrible for this.'

He told the *Daily Mail* that his father had asked him just weeks before whether he believed that the disappearance of Amanda Berry would ever be solved. Anthony replied that he thought Berry was probably dead because she had been missing so long.

'Really? You think so?' his father said, knowing that Berry was locked away in the house at the time.

'If it's true that he took her captive and forced her into having sex with him and having his child and keeping her hidden and keeping them from sunlight, he really took those girls' lives,' Anthony said. 'He doesn't deserve to have his own life anymore. He deserves to be behind bars for the rest of her life. I'm just thankful they're alive.'

Neither Anthony nor his sisters had much of a relationship with their father after their mother had moved out taking them with her. Anthony explained, 'Having that relationship with my dad all these years when we lived in a house where there was domestic violence and I was beaten as well ... we never were really close because of that and it was also something we never really talked about.'

Anthony found it chilling that he had been in the house shortly before the women's release and would have been within a few feet of them. 'It's astonishing to even think about that I was so close to that,' he said. 'That I was physically at the house two weeks ago while that was going on, it's a lot to grasp.'

6

FAMILY
AND FRIENDS

There were other problems in the Castro family. His daughter, Emily, was jailed for attempted murder in 2008 and sentenced to 25 years after she slashed the throat of her 11-month-old daughter Janyla. Emily had just broken up with the child's father when police were called to her home in Fort Wayne, Indiana, after a member of the public reported seeing Emily's mother Grimilda running out into the street with the bleeding baby in her arms. Emily then slashed her own throat and wrists, before trying to drown herself in a creek. Janyla survived and made a full recovery.

It was later revealed that Emily Castro had been to school with Amanda Berry and, at Wilbur Wright Elementary School, had also met Gina DeJesus. Emily had also been in the car with her father moments before he abducted Amanda in 2003. 'I feel so used,' Emily said from her prison cell in Indiana. 'It hurts so bad … I feel like I'm nothing to him. I'm nothing anymore.'

Emily said that her father was a master at keeping secrets, even from his own daughter. After the girls had been abducted, she noticed that the upstairs was blocked off with the big bass speaker. But she figured that, since he lived there alone, he did not have any need for the four bedrooms upstairs. Once she asked whether she could sleep in her old bedroom. He said no. '"It's cold up there, it's blocked off, it's dusty,"' Emily recalled him saying.

After he was arrested, she, too, condemned him. 'He's a monster,' she said. 'Seeing the guy that hugged us … and took us to eat and cared about us supposedly, that he is the guy that is in handcuffs.'

Outside the family, Ariel Castro was thought of as charismatic, a fun guy who always wanted to play with the children in the neighbourhood, often riding his bicycle, or a four-wheel off-roader, and offering youngsters rides up and down the street. Twenty-seven-year-old Juan Perez had lived two houses away from the Castro home since he was five and said that no one in the neighbourhood knew anything about what Castro was up to. Even his Uncle Cesi, a near neighbour, was taken in.

'Apparently he was living two personalities,' Cesi Castro said. The personality that he saw was 'the personality that was dealing with kids and driving the bus, the personality of being a musician and playing the bass.' He was as shocked as anyone.

'Nobody in the neighbourhood or in the family could imagine that something like this would happen,' he said.

He told the *Daily Mail*, 'The DeJesus family and my family

have known each other for a long time and I would like to apologize for what has happened. We are sorry. I am happy for Gina but I am sad that it was one of my relatives. I did not know my nephew – he was the man with two faces.'

Castro listed a local band, Grupo Fuego, as his employers on his Facebook page, but they maintained he had only stood in twice. Band manager Miguel Quinones said he has received hate phone calls and emails since the story broke. He has had to deal with promoters who do not want to have anything to do with a band connected with Castro. But Quinones maintained that Castro only played with the band twice in 2008, and he got rid of him because he was always late. 'He was not an active member of the band,' he said. 'He makes the band look bad. We have been getting emails from people talking negative about the band and the phone calls ... I spoke to the promoters and told them I am talking to the media. The promoters were calling me concerned. I already made a statement on Facebook.'

Quinones, who knows Castro's extended family, said they are devastated by what happened. 'His family is in shock,' he says. 'The uncles are in shock, too. He comes from a great, respectable family in the community. The family has been here for over fifty or sixty years.'

Close friends were also devastated. Castro worked part-time as a mechanic and Rafael Davila met him 20 years ago when he needed some work done on his car. A friend recommended Castro. According to Davila, Castro was helpful and would always fix his car on the cheap. Often, he would sit around and chat while Castro went to work. 'He had aspirations,' Davila said. 'He talked about making money from playing in a band. He was a prince. He was wholesome like John Ritter,' – the actor who stared in ABC's version of the sitcom *Three's Company* – 'I never heard him swear.'

Davila said that Castro was devastated over his divorce, but when he heard the news, he said, 'I thought, it can't be. Now, he is more like a Latino Dr Jekyll and Mr Hyde.'

Castro's Facebook page also says he has five grand-children. A picture showed him in happier times with his daughter Emily and granddaughter Janyla. 'HAPPY BIRTHDAY to my Grand baby Janyla, love the flower on your hair ... I Love You!' he wrote. To all appearances, he was a regular family guy.

'I mean, parents trusted him,' long-term neighbour Juan Perez said. 'He talked to the parents. He was just a regular guy on the street.' But appearances were deceptive. 'He put on that great mask that everyone thought he was a good guy.'

According to Perez, Castro had 'groomed the whole neighbourhood' over the years.

'When my sister was 17, he kept hassling her to take her for a drive in his car on her own,' he said. 'Our mother was very protective so she would not let her do it, but she could have been in that house had she done so.'

Castro was undoubtedly skilled at manipulating people. 'Ariel knew that a lot of people on the block did not have fathers in their families and he took advantage of that,' said Perez. 'He became the father that people did not have. He was so humble, so good at socializing and always around. It was all a game to him, he was just controlling us.'

Perez also said that, in 2010, he and his sister were in their basement when they heard a woman's scream that went on for ten seconds and 'gave them goosebumps'. They called the police but nothing came of it.

In recent years, Uncle Cesi said that Ariel had grown more withdrawn. 'It could have been because of the hiding personality. He had to have two personalities.'

However, Ariel Castro's brother-in-law Juan Alicea had his suspicions. He noticed that Ariel never invited anyone over to the house. 'He'd never had a social life unless they were outside on the porch or something, as far as I know,' Alicea said.

Elsie Cintron, who lives three houses away, said that in 2011 her granddaughter saw a naked woman on a dog lead, crawling in the backyard several years ago and called police. 'But they didn't take it seriously,' she said. She also saw a woman and baby peering out of an upstairs window that was partly boarded up. There was also a report of a figure in an upstairs window pounding on the glass.

Another woman said a friend had told her of 'strange noises … scratching and banging' coming from the house.

Israel Lugo, who lived three doors away from Castro, said he heard pounding on some of the doors of the house in November 2011. Then he heard what he thought was a girl banging on a window. But when he went round to investigate, he saw nothing suspicious. He said he had got 'bad vibes' from Castro and 'didn't want to accuse someone falsely'. But someone must have reported that something odd was going on. According to Lugo, the police had been called to the house several times.

'About two years ago, someone called the police saying they had seen someone inside the property banging on a window,' he said. 'The police showed up but they couldn't get a response so they just thought it was a hoax ... They walked to the side of the house and then left.'

'The police didn't do their job,' said Lupe Collins, who was close to relatives of the abducted women. The police had come in for heavy criticism four years earlier when, in another poverty-stricken part of town, the bodies of 11 women were found in the home and backyard of Anthony Sowell, the 'Cleveland Strangler', who was later convicted of multiple counts of rape, kidnapping and murder, and sentenced to death. The ex-Marine had been convicted of a sex offence earlier and had been released from jail shortly before embarking on his killing spree. He had also had a relationship with the niece of the mayor of Cleveland, Frank Jackson, when she had been a drug addict.

The families of Sowell's victims accused the police of failing to investigate the disappearances properly because most of the victims were poor and addicted to drugs. They were also African-American. For months, the stench of death hung over his house, but it was blamed on a sausage factory next door. He was only caught when a woman escaped from his home during an attempted rape and dialled 911.

Following public outrage over those killings, a panel formed by Mayor Jackson recommended an overhaul of the city's handling of missing-persons and sex-crime investigations. Plainly, more needed to be done.

Confronted again with accusations that police had been indifferent to the plight of women from a poor part of town, senior commanders said that a review of the files found no evidence of complaints by Castro's neighbours. Interviews with the captives confirmed that they were never outside naked and, in ten years, had left the house only twice, wearing wigs, to walk a few steps to the garage. 'They never left the property,' the police said.

Another neighbour, a young man in a stained Cleveland Indians baseball T-shirt, told one newspaper: 'Nobody calls the police around here. You hear screaming every night. You just shrug and turn the TV louder.'

Nevertheless, Perez felt that the local residents shared some of the blame.

'I feel ashamed of myself, my community and this neighbourhood that we didn't see anything.'

Lugo had also seen Castro in the park, playing on the grass with a six-year-old girl, the day before he was arrested. He asked him whose kid it was, and Castro said that she was his girlfriend's daughter. 'I'd only seen Ariel with the little girl on Sunday,' said Lugo. 'We always stop and chat but it was the first time I had seen him with a child. Both his daughters had grown up and left home. When I asked who the little girl was, he said she belonged to his girlfriend and they then walked off to the bakery before I saw them later playing in the park. My own daughter was playing with her, laughing and joking. It is like he didn't have a care in the world. He was just very normal and acting like a family guy.'

Even so, Lugo had misgivings. 'I thought it was a little odd, though, as I've never seen him with a woman since his wife left him, but I didn't question it any further,' he said. 'He used to play bass in the San Lorenzo club on an evening so I just assumed he met his girlfriend there ... Ariel was acting all happy families, like it was his own daughter. They played with my son's girl and he bought her a pastry at the bakery. It was like they were a family. I can't believe it.'

The child, of course, was Castro's daughter by Amanda Berry.

Lugo noticed other strange behaviour. Between his morning and afternoon school runs, Castro would park the bus outside his house. 'He'll go in the house, jump on his motorcycle, take off, come back, jump in the car, take off. Every time he switched a car, he switched an outfit,' he said.

In the basement of the house, the police found ropes and chains where the victims were held initially. Eventually, they were allocated a room upstairs. There were locks on all the doors, but Castro would periodically test his captives by leaving a door ajar, then waiting to pounce if one dared emerge.

The day after Castro's arrest, while a Puerto Rican flag flapped listlessly from a flagpole on the porch, investigators in white hazardous-materials suits arrived to make a detailed search. Outside, a crew hoisted Castro's dirty-brown SUV on to a tow truck as a crowd drawn by the spectacle watched from behind the crime-scene tape less than half a block away.

Nineteen items were removed from the house. One of them was a four-page, handwritten suicide note dated 2004. In it, he claimed that he had been abused as a child and raped. It also provided details about the capture of each of his victims. It was their own fault, he maintained. The women had disobeyed a golden rule, he said. 'They are here against their will because they made the mistake of getting in a car with a total stranger.'

The note was written after the abduction of Gina DeJesus. 'I don't know why I kept looking for another,' he wrote. 'I already had two in my possession.' He added, 'I am a sexual predator. I need help.'

Psychologists described the note as a 'purging' of feelings of guilt and thought it was never intended for publication. He also asked for his money to be divided among his victims once he was dead.

Federal agents also searched a vacant house nearby. They would only say their search was an attempt to get evidence in the case against Castro, but they refused to say what they found or what led them there.

Mary Myers, an associate professor of criminal justice and retired police captain, speculated that the captives must eventually have formed some kind of functioning relationship with Castro. 'The victims depend on this person; they want to please this person,' said Myers. 'The suspect in turn wants to be loved and to dominate the victims.'

Jeff Gardere, a clinical psychologist, also speculated that Castro may have effectively assigned different roles to each of his captives – the prettiest one as a 'sex toy', another as 'the genetic pool for his offspring' and the third to be 'mother to the other women'.

Dr Kris Mohandie, a forensic psychologist who has been a consultant in other long-term kidnapping cases said, 'These are some of the most catastrophic kinds of experiences a human being can be subjected to ...' The perpetrators of similar crimes have been men 'who have had longstanding fantasies of capturing, controlling, abusing and dominating women'. Such men, he said, use a perverse system of rewards and punishments to create fear and submission in their victims, who quickly lose all sense of self and become dependent on their captors. 'Total control over another human being is what stimulates them,' he said.

In an interview with the *Daily Mail*, Anthony Castro said that he had spoken to members of the family since the arrest and, after getting over the shock of the gravity of the allegations, they had all accepted that Ariel Castro was capable of holding the three women against their will. 'They're furious,' he said. 'They're livid.' However, Anthony found it hard to believe that the three women were kept in the house for the entire ten years.

Ariel Castro's brothers, 54-year-old Pedro and 50-year-old Onil, were also arrested, but no charges were brought against them. Onil also owned his own house and had two sons with a live-in girlfriend of 15 years' standing. The boys were then in their twenties. The girlfriend had moved out some ten years earlier and Onil then lived alone just a few blocks from Ariel. But while Ariel's house was rundown, Onil's was painted light pink and was the nicest house on the block.

Like Ariel, Onil valued his privacy. There were signs on the gate saying there was a guard dog and warning people not to trespass. He used to entertain in the garden at the back. There was a swing on the lawn, a picnic table and two easy chairs where Onil would drink with friends. A visiting reporter noticed in the hedge a bottle of Ronrico, a cheap rum that cost just $11 a litre.

'They would have get-togethers and they would be drinking out there. They used to have dogs,' said 13-year-old Zamira Webb who lived opposite. 'I used to see one of the guys in the top window always looking out at me as I walked past.'

Pedro lived with their mother, who had become a Jehovah's Witness, and rode a bicycle around the neighbourhood in the summer. One neighbour said he was good-natured and helpful around the neighbourhood. 'I was very surprised when I heard,' she said. 'You never really know who your neighbours are.'

Pedro turned from being top of the class to a hopeless alcoholic in his teens. Former schoolmates said that he was drunk '24/7' and would walk around with no shoes drinking litre bottles of strong rum that he knocked back in two swigs. 'Pedro was a straight-A student until he started drinking,' said 58-year-old Nester Roman who went to school with Pedro. 'He used to help me with my homework, but I was the one who finished my diploma and not him in the end. He guzzled a pint of rum in two shots. He also liked wine and Mad Dog 20/20. Pedro used to be a biker and he was really into his bikes, but now he just drinks. If any of them was going to be a bad influence, it would be him. He was into craziness. He and Onil have been boozing it up for years. That's all they do.'

Onil drank nearly as much as his older brother. He never acknowledged his neighbours and never smiled. 'Onil never talked to nobody,' said neighbour Ailsa Laboy. 'He didn't even say hi or bye or nothing. His head was always down. He never even managed a smile.'

The three brothers were close. Ms Laboy said, 'I remember on Sunday that Pedro and Onil were out there in front of the house acting really casual. It was about 5.30pm. Ariel came out to speak to them at one point then went back into the house.'

'My dad's brothers were the two closest people to him,'

Anthony told the *Daily Mail*. 'My dad's a really private person. If anybody knew what he was doing, it would be those two.' But there was no suggestion that there was any collusion between them. 'My dad is the most ... he is the strongest and most able-bodied out of them,' Anthony said. 'My two uncles are frail. They've drunk themselves into terrible health.' Both men had been alcoholics for years. Their police records also showed that they had been pummelling each other over the years. However, Onil had eventually sobered up. 'When I was a kid, he was always drunk,' said Anthony. 'Both of them, my uncles were always drunk.' His uncle Pedro was so wasted by alcohol it was hard to carry on a conversation with him. 'Every time I went to visit my grandmother, he always just seemed be lying on his bed, watching TV,' said Anthony. 'He was there every time.'

7

HOUSE OF HORRORS

Although Ariel Castro's house looked ordinary enough, if a little run down, it did give cause for suspicion. At the top of the house at the back, there was a smashed window, thought to have been broken in an attempt to attract attention or, perhaps, to wriggle out to freedom. It was from this window that a neighbour said she once saw a little girl looking out.

The back windows of the house were either boarded up or had the curtains drawn; even the large garage in the back garden had its windows covered. There was a small tent-like structure and a rusty basketball hoop standing at an angle. Round the 8ft by 12ft back yard, Castro had built a stockade. Using chicken wire and a blue tarpaulin, he had made an 8ft fence. He had also let the trees and bushes grow so overgrown that no one could see in. This was reminiscent of the back garden where California captive

Jaycee Lee Dugard was held and brought up her two daughters.

Israel Lugo gave a description of the house: 'Inside the house, there is a staircase up when you go in,' he said, 'and behind it there is one going down. On the second floor, there are four bedrooms, and then there's the attic at the top ... From what I gather, they were being held in separate rooms, not just the basement.'

The house was in a tough neighbourhood that was struggling with unemployment and poverty; there were few well-tended houses. Several houses, including an apartment building down the block from Castro's residence, were vacant and boarded up, and there were a number of vacant lots.

It seems that Castro used to be seen at the property very often, but in recent years had only been seen there a few times a week. Neighbours began to believe that the property was vacant and that he was only holding on to it as an investment. This would have meant that the girls trapped inside would have had to wait for days at a time to eat.

But one neighbour remembered late-night deliveries of groceries, while another remarked on the porch light that burned all night, even though many of the windows were boarded up. 'Why would an abandoned house have a porch light on?' he recalled thinking.

Another visitor was fellow musician Ricky Sanchez. They would share a meal and jam salsa songs during his frequent visits to Castro's home. 'I'm sure they heard me,' said Sanchez.

He first visited the house in 2001 and his last visit was on 2 May 2013, four days before the women were released.

Sanchez said the living room was a mess. He also went upstairs where there was a broken-down bed frame with a misshapen mattress. There were half-a-dozen deadbolt locks on each exterior door. The security system was so tight that Sanchez needed help letting himself out. Castro explained that he needed such a high level of security to protect his musical instruments.

And when Sanchez heard thumping noises from the walls, Castro assured him it was just his boisterous dogs. On his last visit, he was even introduced to six-year-old Jocelyn. The child was shy and Castro hustled her out of the kitchen, saying she was his granddaughter.

Gina DeJesus's uncle Tito, who played in bands with Castro over the preceding 20 years, also recalled visiting Castro's house. But he did not notice anything out of the ordinary. Later, he realized that he was only feet away from his captive niece.

Another long-term friend, Richard Caraballo, said, 'It's hard to process that these girls were in the basement when I was staying in the back yard, and they did not make a sound.'

Otherwise, Castro left no clue. 'He lived normally,' Caraballo said. 'Everything looked normal. There was nothing to question. It was a normal house.'

Richard was a cousin of Castro's wife Grimilda and knew that the relationship was abusive. 'He was pretty dominant toward women,' said Caraballo, but 'as a friend, he was a great friend.' Castro loved hot rods and taught Caraballo how to drive. He also loved his music. 'He played in a band, especially jazz and salsa,' said Caraballo, who moved to West Palm Beach in 1998, saying that the friendship had changed two years before Castro was arrested. He was visiting from Florida with his two children around Christmas, and he noticed plastic covering the windows at Castro's house. 'He greeted us at the front door and told us to go to the back,' Caraballo said. Castro wouldn't let him and his family inside, which he thought was strange.

Caraballo also thought if anyone knew the real Ariel Castro, it was him. But now, he said, 'You put the puzzle together, and you see what actually created this monster.'

Fifty-three-year-old Richard Cuevas, who claimed to have known the Castro brothers, said that violence ran in the family. He told the *New York Daily News* that the brothers' father, Sesa Castro, was a vicious gambler who 'wasn't any man to play around with … He was always at the pool hall playing numbers,' Cuevas said. 'Everybody knew not to cross him … if he wanted to make you disappear, you would disappear.' And there were rumours that Sesa Castro had mob ties, Cuevas said.

As kids, Ariel looked up to Pedro and Pedro looked out for Ariel. Ariel was quieter, said Cuevas, who graduated from Lincoln West High with Ariel in 1979.

Apart from being a talented musician, the former school bus driver was a gifted baseball player and used to play with the neighbourhood kids at Seymour Park and Lincoln West Park. 'But never in my wildest dreams did I think that kid would grow up to be like this.'

Former Spanish-language TV anchor woman Daisy Cortes had known Ariel Castro ten years before his arrest when her fiancé, Robert Ocasio, led a band called the Latin Jazz Project. Castro played bass with the group. She was shocked when she heard that the house he lived in was a pigsty. 'It was strange,' she said, 'because he was always very professional and well kept. He didn't look like the kind of person who lived like that.' Then, around 2003, Castro began missing a lot of rehearsals and shows. 'He always had excuses, saying he didn't feel well,' she said. 'Now we know why he didn't show up.'

Cortes said she left Cleveland in 2005 after Ocasio was killed in a car crash. Castro was sympathetic. 'He was the first one who called to offer condolences,' she said. 'I needed the support.' Now she thinks he was trying to worm his way into her life. 'He tried to get close to the family,' she said. 'Thinking back, he was very weird. He would play the bass by himself. He was always solitary. He never spoke much. He just looked at you. He would communicate with his eyes, squinting. There was no emotion there.'

But in 2003, Castro seems to have taken a fancy to Cortez's nine-year-old daughter Bianca Cruz, during the set break at an outdoor concert. 'He was touching her hair,' she said. 'He looked like a nice person, the kind of person who smiles with his eyes.'

At the time, Bianca did not think anything of Castro stroking her hair, but ten years later Daisy Cortes said, 'It's awful. My daughter could have been a victim.'

Bianca Cruz said, 'I didn't think he was doing it in a bad way back then. In the Hispanic culture, it's normal to touch someone's hair.' However, Cortes said she once considered hiring Castro to give music lessons to Bianca and Roberto, her nine-year-old son by Ocasio. 'Thank God I never invited him over to teach my children,' she said.

Fifty-eight-year-old Zaida Delgado, a long-time family friend, said that she had also been aware of Castro's darker side. 'There was something not right about him,' she said. 'He could be flaky and off the wall. He was also arrogant, like "I am Mr Cool … I am the best". He had an attitude, like "I am God's gift".'

But most local criticism was reserved for the authorities. 'The Cleveland Police should be ashamed of themselves,' said Yolanda Asia, an assistant manager of a nearby store. 'These girls were five minutes away. They were looking for years and years. They were right under their nose.'

It is thought that police were within earshot of the victims more than a thousand times while they were held captive. From the time when the first kidnap victim vanished in August 2002 until Amanda Berry and her daughter emerged on 6 May 2013, the police responded to 1,099 calls on that block. That is, once every three-and-a-half days. Residents at Number 2003 Seymour Avenue, the house next door, called the police 35 times. The police were called to Number 2115, a couple of doors down the road, 37 times and Number 2120, across the street and a few doors down, 68 times. NBC News, who unearthed the figures, said, 'The neighbourhood emerges from the police records as a central character in the crime story, a declining neighbourhood in social turmoil. Why would the quiet house on the block draw a second glance from officers who are responding to domestic abuse calls and flashers, to broken windows and prowlers, to a fight involving 20 people armed with baseball bats?'

While some residents described the neighbourhood as close-knit, others said it has suffered from increasing drug use and violent crime. To indicate the current state of the neighbourhood, Khalid Samad, a community organizer in

Cleveland who had worked with police and established community searches for the missing women, described an incident that occurred the evening that the women were released. 'Not an hour after they're out, I'm standing on the street near the Castro house and a fight broke out a few doors down because a guy who was out there saw a guy who he recognized as having shot him on the street,' Samad said. 'Dude took off running, and they're wrestling down in front of the church. That's the kind of thing that would go on there.'

Three days after Michelle Knight disappeared on 22 August 2002, police visited a house two doors away from the Castro's. They were responding to a call at 2221 Seymour Avenue about the theft of a cell phone. Nine days after Amanda Berry disappeared on 21 April 2003, police visited 2221 Seymour Avenue again, this time over a car with no plates that had been left on the street for months. And the day after Gina DeJesus disappeared on 2 April 2004, police were at 2022 Seymour Avenue, investigating harassing telephone calls.

Some incidents put officers right outside Castro's front door. On 6 April 2007, two cars collided almost directly in front of his house. The police were on the scene for 78 minutes. On Independence Day weekend in 2006, there was a street fight near 2115 Seymour Avenue involving 20 people with baseball bats. Several police cars raced to the scene and a pregnant woman was taken to the hospital.

Then there were the two incidents when officers came to Castro's house during the 3,910 nights that Michelle Knight was missing. The first was over the child he left in the school bus while he went to have lunch in Wendy's.

Then, on 3 July 2009, Castro called the police to complain about a fight outside on the street. There is some confusion over this in the police record. The police maintain that there is no indication that they were remiss or overlooked clues that would have led to the discovery of the women. They responded to reports of unidentified women screaming, but there was no indication that the screams came from Castro's house.

On 20 January 2003, five months after Michelle Knight had gone missing, a visually impaired woman at 2115 Seymour Avenue, just three doors from Castro's house, reported hearing a female 'screaming out front'. An officer arrived within five minutes, and was on the scene for 45 minutes. But there was no indication in the records of what was found.

Then, on 6 May 2008, while all three women were in Castro's house, the same woman heard a female voice at the apartment building across the street from her house, yelling, 'Get off me!' The caller said the voice sounded covered or muffled. She also said she heard a baby crying. The dispatch log does not indicate that police found anything. The officer was on the scene for minutes, but no report of the investigation was filed.

There was no support in the records for statements by a neighbour who – after the women were rescued – claimed to have reported strange goings-on at the Castro house. There was no record, for example, of a witness saying they had seen a woman chained and naked in the back yard.

Police officials insist that these reports were never made. The victims themselves told investigators they were only allowed outside twice, and then forced to wear wigs and sunglasses and keep their heads down. 'There is no evidence to indicate that any of them were ever outside in the yard, in chains, without clothing, or any other manner,' said Martin Flask, Cleveland Director of Public Safety.

Police Chief Michael McGrath also insisted that the police had no record of anyone calling to report anything suspicious about the Castro house. He told NBC's *Today* show that he was absolutely sure that, over the years, the police did everything they could to find the missing women. 'We have no record of those calls coming in over the past ten years,' he said.

'I can tell you personally that I busted my butt to find those girls,' Keith Sulzer, Cleveland Police District Commander, told a community meeting. 'Me and my guys searched every vacant lot, every vacant building, every-where that we could legally go in and search.'

The very absence of these reports speaks volumes about the state of terrorized isolation the women were kept in. Although they were eventually released from their chains in the basement and allowed to move upstairs, Castro intimidated them, beating them savagely if they cried for help or attempted to escape. Law enforcement sources told local station WOIO that Castro would 'play this little dangerous game that he would tell the women he was about to leave the home, and then he would wait and, if one of them tried to open that door, he would go in and attack them. That was one of the ways he was able to keep them there.'

Even so, Samad, the community organizer, said he believed the women's captivity might not have gone unnoticed in a more affluent neighbourhood. 'If this was an inner-ring suburban neighbourhood,' he said, 'you'd have some nosy neighbours who would ask, "Why are your windows boarded up ... why are you taking groceries in if you don't have family there?"'

8

IN CAPTIVITY

Ariel Castro waived his Miranda rights – his right to remain silent and have an attorney present during his interrogation – and gave the police a detailed statement after his arrest. Michelle Knight, Amanda Berry and Gina DeJesus also provided statements in due course. 'What the suspect told us and what the young ladies told us ... what they told law enforcement was key,' Deputy Police Chief Ed Tomba said. 'That's the major part of the case.'

Audio tapes of the police officer's shocked response to what they found in Castro's home were also released. 'This might be for real,' an officer said at 5.55pm on 6 May, adding a minute later, 'There might be others in the house ... Georgina DeJesus might be in this house also.' Then at 5.58pm, he radioed, 'We found them! We found them!' A woman could be heard sobbing in the background. The officer then said, 'We also have a Michelle Knight in the house. I don't know if you want to look that up in the system. Thirty-two years old.'

Officer Anthony Espada said later that, when he called dispatchers to report that the women had been found and were safe, he struggled to get the words out. 'I've broke down a few times on the scene and in private since then,' Espada said. 'Those three girls are my heroes ... after what they went through in that house all those years.' The rescue had a profound effect on Espada. 'I can still picture us just pulling up, seeing Amanda – couldn't believe it,' he said. 'I just keep replaying and replaying it every day since it happened.'

When they arrived at the house, it was his partner who recognized the long-missing woman. 'Just the emotion from that point, that he confirmed it was Amanda, was overwhelming,' Espada said. More was to come when he found Michelle Knight upstairs. 'She came charging at me. She's like, "You saved us! You saved us!"' he recalled. 'And I'm holding on to her so tight. And then, within a few seconds, I see another girl come out of the bedroom.'

Other police officers who helped free the captives also spoke out. 'When I heard there were people in the house, I ran up to the door, but it was locked from the inside,' Officer Michael Simon said. 'So I grabbed the handrail by the stairs to use as a prying tool ... but the other officers kicked the door in. Once inside, I felt evil in the house.'

Officer Michael Tracy said, 'We've all seen the flyers for Amanda and Gina, but I was experiencing both disbelief and excitement when I saw Amanda in the window. Our first thought was to safely get inside, make sure the girls were okay, and then get them out.'

IN CAPTIVITY

Officer Barbara Johnson said Michelle Knight embraced her when she saw her. 'Michelle hugged me first, then clutched me and said, "Don't let me go." You can't really describe how I felt ... It rips the heart out of my chest.' Johnson then spent the next six hours at the hospital with the women after their rescue. She said that nothing in her training could have prepared her for the wrenching emotions she felt.

'You try and forget about this, but you can't ever forget something like this,' she said.

Castro was held on an $8 million bond. Judge Lauren Moore calculated bail at $2 million per victim; that included six-year-old Jocelyn, whose DNA testing proved was Castro's daughter. Castro's DNA was also compared against samples taken from other Ohio crime scenes, but there was no match.

Castro's attorney had sought a more manageable bail, telling the judge Castro was a long-time resident of Cleveland with no prior felony convictions and had limited financial resources as he was living off an unemployment cheque. Even the prosecutor had only asked for bail to be set at $5 million, even though Castro put the women through a 'horrifying ordeal' that included repeated beatings and sexual assaults, and periods of being bound and restrained inside Castro's home. Throughout the hearing, Castro kept his eyes lowered and his chin tucked into the zipped top of a dark-blue jacket. At times, he appeared to be chewing on the collar. He did not speak, looked down at the ground for nearly the entire proceedings and signed documents with his hands still handcuffed.

Afterwards, Cuyahoga County Prosecutor Timothy

McGinty told reporters that aggravated murder charges could be filed in connection with miscarriages that the police said one of the abducted women suffered when Castro used force to terminate her pregnancies after repeatedly raping her. 'The law of Ohio calls for the death penalty for those most depraved criminals who commit aggravated murder during the course of a kidnapping,' McGinty said.

Initially, Castro had only been charged with four counts of kidnapping and three counts of rape, but McGinty said he would face justice for every act of sexual violence, assault and other crimes against the women. This meant that the counts could be in the hundreds, he said. 'This child kidnapper operated a torture chamber and private prison in the heart of our city,' said McGinty. 'The horrific brutality and torture that the victims endured for a decade is beyond comprehension. My office will also engage in a formal process in which we evaluate whether to seek charges eligible for the death penalty. Capital punishment must be reserved for those crimes that are truly the worst examples of human conduct.' In Ohio, the death penalty was administered by lethal injection.

Castro was kept under close scrutiny behind bars. He was on suicide watch and monitored every ten minutes. All movements of the prisoners had to be reported to the shift sergeant who noted them in the jail logs, and two guards had to accompany him whenever he was out of his cell. The log notes, 'Castro is a high-profile inmate; very high media attention.'

While on remand in Cuyahoga County Jail, Castro spent most of the last few days lying on a mat in his cell or on his bunk, occasionally walking around the cell naked and staring in the mirror. The logs also recorded that he drank Kool-Aid and complained that it was cold when he first arrived. Later, he refused to have a shower because he had a headache. The guards had to stop him using loose strings ripped from the floor mat as dental floss. The media noted that the tables had turned. The captor was now the captive – and he was going crazy. He was also the target of ceaseless abuse from other inmates. 'They were screaming at him all night,' said a prisoner who was released the next day. 'He was just laying there, taking it. They were saying, "Don't feed that rapist! He doesn't deserve any respect!"'

The former inmate said he walked past Ariel Castro's cell and asked if he was the one who did it. 'Ariel shook his head ... yes,' he said.

Warrants were issued for the arrest of Castro's two brothers. They gave themselves up and were cleared of any wrongdoing after three days. 'There is nothing that leads us to believe that they were involved or they had any knowledge of this,' said Deputy Police Chief Tomba. 'Ariel kept everybody at a distance.' However, the brothers were also heckled by fellow inmates at the Central Prison Unit at Cleveland Police Headquarters.

After Castro's two brothers were released, they told CNN that they hoped Ariel would rot in jail. 'The monster is a goner,' said Onil. He also hoped that his brother would not be given the death penalty, but rather be sentenced to life imprisonment as he would suffer more that way. 'I don't even want them to take his life like that,' he said. 'I want him to suffer in that jail to the last extent. I don't care if they even feed him.'

THE DISAPPEARED

To his brothers, Ariel no longer existed; it was as if he was dead and they were happy that his victims had survived. 'I'm glad he left the door open,' said Onil, who also even speculated that Ariel had might left the door unlocked on purpose. After harbouring the secret for so many years, perhaps Ariel wanted to get caught. 'Maybe his time was up,' Onil said. 'Maybe he was inside too much ... he wanted to get caught. But if he did it that way, he shouldn't of went to Mama's house and picked me up and put me in a car, if he knows that was going to happen.'

Onil had been to their mother's house, too, and had cadged a lift off Ariel on the day he had been arrested. After their arrest, the three brothers were held in separate cells, but Onil saw Ariel as he walked passed on the way to the lavatory. 'When he walked past me, he goes, "Onil, you're never going to see me again. I love you, bro." And that was it,' Onil said. 'And he put his fist up for a bump. He goes, "Onil, I'm sorry. You didn't know nothing about this, Onil. I'm sorry, Onil." And that was it.' The last time Onil saw Ariel, he seemed resigned to his fate, he said.

Over the previous ten years, Pedro and Onil had rarely visited their brother's house. When they did go inside, they never went past the kitchen. The rest of the house was screened off by curtains and the radio or TV was always blaring to drown out any other noise. 'He always stayed to himself with his music,' Onil told CNN. 'Mama use to say, "Check your brother. Check on your brother. He lives alone in that house. He's a loner." So I would text him and he would text me back: "I'm fine."'

The brothers insisted that Ariel would not have been fine if they had known what was going on. Pedro said he would have grabbed his brother by the neck and reported him to the police – 'brother or no brother'. On air, they apologized to Michelle, Amanda and Gina. 'I'm sorry you had to go through this,' said Pedro. 'I was thinking about you girls being missing. I am just grateful that they are home and free, out of that horrible house. I'm sorry for what Ariel done.'

Pedro had known Felix DeJesus, Gina's father, for a long time. When he heard that Ariel had Gina, he broke down. 'Ariel, you got his daughter,' Pedro said on TV. 'You even went to the vigils. You had posters. You give his mama a hug. And you got his daughter captive.'

Onil said he wanted the families to get justice to the fullest extent. 'This has torn my heart apart. This has killed me. I am a walking corpse right now,' Onil concluded.

Castro's daughter Arlene, who now lives in Indiana, also went on television to apologize to Gina, the girl who was once her best friend. 'I am absolutely so, so sorry,' said the 22-year-old. 'I really want to see Gina and I want you to meet my kids. I'm so sorry for everything.' She said that she and her father were never that close and, when she visited the house, she never saw any trace of the captured women. 'Every time we would talk it would just be short conversations, just a "Hello, how are you doin'?" and "Let me know if you need anything" and that was it,' she said. She added that she was disgusted by what he had done and said she wanted nothing to do with him anymore. 'I have no problem cutting him out of my life,' she said. 'I have no problem doing that. I never want to see him again.' Nevertheless, she had a series of questions for him, in addition to the main one – 'Why did you do this?'

'Another thing I would like to ask him is, when did you think this was going to be over? How did you think it was going to end? You're fifty-two years old. Did you think you could carry on this charade for ever?' She also insisted that Castro's actions were no reflection on the rest of the family.

Castro's mother Lillian Rodriguez was also apologetic. Outside Onil's home, she expressed her sorrow to the mothers of the three women her son had imprisoned, raped and abused. 'I ask for forgiveness from those mothers, that the girls will forgive me,' she said in Spanish. 'I have a son who is sick, who has committed something serious. I am sorry for what my son has done.'

Before Castro's arrest she had often been seen going to church or gardening outside her Cleveland home. But with her son inside, she hid behind locked doors and, when confronted by the press, appeared overwrought.

Back in Puerto Rico, in the small mountain hamlet of Duey, 8 miles south of San Juan, which Ariel left 40 years earlier, the extended family were also grappling to come to terms with what he had done. 'We don't know what kind of demon he had in him to do what he did,' said 56-year-old cousin Aida Castro. 'A demon inside him made him lose his mind … [but] he is still blood, family.'

As a consequence, the family were being treated as pariahs. Castro's 63-year-old aunt Monserrate Baez said she was terrified by the look on her nephew's face when it appeared on the front page of the local paper. 'He looks menacing,' she said. 'We don't know how he could have done what he did.'

Through it all, the family clung together. 'Most of us are good,' said 48-year-old cousin Javier Castro. 'One person can't shame an entire family … we won't let it. I wish I could say we aren't cousins. We are good people, even if he's evil.'

Before Castro's arrest, the family's summit of shame came when his mother Lillian and Pedro, his father, split up. Pedro stayed behind in Puerto Rico while the rest of his family, including ten-year-old Ariel, relocated to Cleveland. 'Maybe that's what messed up Ariel,' said 76-year-old Duey-resident Hilberto Caraballo, who knew Castro's parents. 'When you are crazy, you need any excuse, I guess.' However, Caraballo said that Pedro was a good father to Ariel before the break-up.

On 12 June 2013, Ariel Castro pleaded not guilty to an initial 329-count indictment. Again, he kept his head bowed throughout the proceedings. Attorneys for the victims told the court that they wanted to get the case to court as quickly as possible, so they could put the whole thing behind them. 'The longer this process lasts, the more painful it is for them. And the more sordid details of this horror that get disclosed in this process, the more painful it is for them,' said Kathy Joseph, representing Michelle Knight.

James Wooley, attorney for Amanda Berry and Gina DeJesus, said, 'They have faith in the process, but the simple, honest truth is they would like it to be over. They want this whole thing behind them. Any date by which this may end is like light at the end of a tunnel.'

The judge also ruled at the hearing that there would be no blogging or the use of other electronic media from inside the courtroom.

On 3 July, Castro was deemed mentally fit to stand trial after a two-hour examination. In court, he again hung his head. He murmured answers to the Cuyahoga County Judge

Michael Russo's questions with simple phrases, never saying more than a few words. When asked whether he understood why he had undergone a mental evaluation, he said, 'Yes.' He was most eloquent when he asked to see Jocelyn, the six-year-old daughter he had fathered by Amanda Berry. The prosecution voiced their objections and visitation rights were denied. 'I just think that it would be inappropriate,' said Judge Russo.

After the hearing, Castro's attorney Jaye Schlachet told WKYC-TV, 'I can tell you that Mr Castro is extremely committed to the well-being and positive future for his daughter, whom he loves dearly. And if people find that to be a disconnect from what he's alleged to have done, then the people will just have to deal with it. We just know how he feels about his little girl.' Schlachet also gave details of Castro's captivity. 'He's watched completely … he has a window through his door. He doesn't have a television, doesn't have radio, doesn't have magazines, no access to newspapers. He's completely isolated from society.'

Another of Castro's lawyers, Craig Weintraub, told the TV station, 'The initial portrayal by the media has been one of a "monster", and that's not the impression that I got when I talked to him for three hours. I know that family members who have been interviewed by the media have expressed that as well.'

Prosecutor Tim McGinty said he was determined to prove them wrong. 'You'll make the same logical judgement when you see the facts,' he said. 'You have not seen the evidence yet.'

Ariel Castro appeared in court again on 17 July to plead not guilty to fresh charges. He now stood accused of 512 counts of kidnapping, 446 counts of rape and a half-dozen counts of felonious assault. He had already been arraigned on charges of aggravated murder, a law that covered 'the unlawful termination of another's pregnancy'. The fresh charges brought the total count up to 977. The indictment went into some detail; it said that Castro had held the women captive, sometimes chaining them to a pole in a basement, to a bedroom heater or inside a van. One woman was forced to wear a motorcycle helmet while chained in the basement and, when she tried to escape, he wrapped the cord from a vacuum cleaner around her neck.

Castro had lured Michelle Knight into his Cleveland home with the promise of a puppy for her son; another victim was enticed by an invitation to meet his daughter. All three victims were locked in his vehicle in his garage for three days when a visitor stayed over.

The women kept diaries that documented their lives as captives and the abuse they suffered. According to a court memorandum, 'The entries speak of forced sexual conduct, of being locked in a dark room, of anticipating the next session of abuse, of the dreams of someday escaping and being reunited with family, of being chained to a wall, of being held like a prisoner of war ... of being treated like an animal.'

Amanda Berry's diary was addressed to her mother. After her mum died, she continued writing to her mother in heaven, 'seeking to soothe her', she said. Meanwhile, she prayed for deliverance and for the health of her daughter, whom Castro had fathered. The diaries, the memorandum said, showed how 'the victims had to watch the rest of the world turn as they were held in captivity ... Holidays, world events, and even the passing of Ms Berry's mother were observed by them, removed from the outside world.'

The sentencing memorandum also said that Castro kept his captives chained by the ankle and fed them only one meal a day. He 'admits his disgusting and inhuman conduct' but 'remains remorseless for his actions'. Castro said that he had no exit strategy from his complicated double life and finally gave the women a chance to escape by leaving a door unlocked.

Michelle Knight was forced to abort a pregnancy by doing strenuous exercise while being deprived of food and given only tea. She then had to deliver Amanda Berry's child by herself and resuscitate the baby after birth. Castro had threatened to kill her if she failed. Afterwards, he raped her. The document also said that the three women were not allowed out of their bedroom to go to the lavatory, and had to use plastic toilets which were emptied infrequently. There were few other amenities. In the room where Michelle Knight and Gina DeJesus were held, a clock radio was found alongside their chains. And in the room Amanda Berry shared with her daughter, stuffed animals lined the bed and crayon drawings were found taped to the wall. One of them was a homemade birthday card.

Castro deliberately kept the basement freezing cold and made the attic unbearably hot so he could punish his prisoners if they should show any signs of resistance. He also kept them in a state of terror by telling them that he was 'hunting for replacements'. He claimed he had previously captured other victims who had subsequently been disposed of. The letters 'R.I.P.' were scrawled on the wall, and he menaced his captives with a gun.

IN CAPTIVITY

The women were kept 'in a state of powerlessness' through physical, sexual and psychological violence. 'He made them believe that their physical survival depended on him, and he threatened to end their lives if they did not comply with his every demand,' the memorandum said, the purpose of which was to serve as justification for Castro's sentence should it come under review at any time in the future.

While in court, Castro again dropped his head and closed his eyes. This time, Judge Pamela Barker would have none of it. 'Mr Castro, would you please look at me, sir,' she said. 'I need to make sure you understand what I am saying.'

Castro raised his head, but only opened his eyes momentarily and the judge had to repeat the request. 'Mr Castro again, you must look at me, sir,' she said. 'Can you open your eyes, please?'

'I'm trying,' responded Castro as he lowered his head and closed his eyes again, remaining that way throughout the court appearance.

9

AFTER
THE ORDEAL

When Michelle Knight, Amanda Berry, Gina DeJesus and Amanda's six-year-old daughter Jocelyn were released from Castro's house, they were taken to MetroHealth Medical Center where they were found to be suffering from severe dehydration and malnourishment. Throughout their captivity, they had received no medical treatment. However, the authorities said that they seemed to be healthy, despite being in need of a good meal.

Dr Gerald Maloney said, 'This isn't the ending we usually hear to these stories, so we're very happy. We're very happy for them.' Normally, women who have been abducted are found dead.

The women were able to speak to hospital staff and police were able to confirm their identities. Before their abduction, all three had lived within two miles of the suspect's home. A spokesman for the DeJesus family said,

'In all this time – ten years – nobody never figured nothing about where she was at and this has come to an end and it's right here on Seymour.'

Her cousin Sylvia Colon said Gina's mother Nancy Ruiz had never given up hope of finding her alive. 'She has always said that she just could feel it, a link a mom can feel, but she always believed Gina was alive and well,' she said. Speaking to the press on Mother's Day the following week, she added, 'I just want to say what a phenomenal Mother's Day gift she gets.'

Outside the hospital, Gina's childhood friend Kayla Rogers said, 'I've been praying, never forgot about her, ever. This is amazing. This is a celebration. I'm so happy. I just want to see her walk out of those doors so I can hug her.'

Praising the captive women's strength, Gina's aunt Sandra Ruiz said, 'What we've done in ten years is nothing compared to what those women have done in ten years to survive.'

Amanda Berry wept as she was reunited with sister Beth Serrano at the hospital. Her cousin Tasheena Mitchell said she could not wait to have Amanda in her arms. 'I'm going to hold her, and I'm going to squeeze her and I probably won't let her go,' she said.

Cleveland's Director of Public Safety, Martin Flask, said the endings of most missing-person cases were 'usually tragic'. In this case, though, 'all of us are excited and pleased with the outcome. But when you look at what we suspect they experienced, our joy is tempered.' And Stephen Anthony, head of the FBI in Cleveland, said, 'Prayers have finally been answered. The nightmare is over. These three young ladies have provided us with the ultimate definition of survival and perseverance. The healing can now begin.'

But Cleveland's mayor Frank Jackson took a more pragmatic view. He said the investigation into the women's abductions had only just begun and there were several key unanswered questions: 'Why were they taken, who took them and how did they remain undetected for so long?'

Amanda Berry and Gina DeJesus were released the following morning, while Michelle Knight remained in hospital for further medical attention. Her 62-year-old grandmother Deborah Knight said, 'When she was severely beaten, he had beat her so bad in the face she has to have facial reconstruction, and she's lost hearing in one ear.'

There were loud cheers when Amanda arrived at her sister's home that afternoon with her daughter Jocelyn and a police escort. The front porch was festooned with balloons, cards and teddy bears. A large sign read 'Welcome Home, Amanda', while another read 'We Never Lost Hope, Mandy'. A huge crowd jostled to get a glimpse of Amanda as she went in through the back of the house. Amanda's sister thanked the public for their support, but asked for privacy. And her grandfather Troy Berry had a special gift for her – before Amanda went missing, her grandfather promised her his limited edition Chevy Monte Carlo from 1986, the year she was born. All these years later, Amanda remembered that promise.

'That's the first thing she asked: "Have you still got my car?"' said Troy. 'It lit up her world when I told her it's still sitting here.' He had kept the car in his driveway for the last ten years. Following Amanda's release, local body shops stepped in to restore it.

Jocelyn was introduced to the family and there was an instant rapport between Troy and his new granddaughter. 'She jumped on my lap and said, "Papaw, give me a hug,"' Troy said. 'She is so smart. Amanda said she taught her a lot at home when Castro wasn't around.'

That afternoon, Gina DeJesus arrived home in the afternoon to chants of 'Gina! Gina!' With a bright-yellow-hooded sweatshirt pulled over her face, she gave a thumbs-up to the cheering crowd. Protection was provided by the Guardian Angels sporting their distinctive red berets. She, too, was greeted with balloons tied to the front fence and a banner that read, 'Welcome home, Gina'. Her father Felix pumped the air with his fist and hugged relatives and cops. 'This will be the best Mother's Day present any mother could hope for,' he said.

Her mother Nancy Ruiz did not disagree. 'The only thing I did was grab her and hug her,' she told the crowd. 'Until this moment, I still pinch myself.' Ruiz said she also got a chance to meet the two other women her daughter was trapped with – Michelle Knight and Amanda Berry. But seeing her daughter was just so sweet, she said. 'That first moment, it was awesome,' she said, choking up. She also thanked those who had helped the family over the past nine years. 'Even the ones that doubted, I want to thank them the most,' she said. 'They're the ones that made me stronger, the ones that made me feel the most that my daughter was out there.'

Earlier, Sandra Ruiz made an unexpected plea to well-wishers. 'As a community, do not go retaliate against the family of the suspect,' she said. Indeed, she told ABC's *20/20* show that she was prepared to forgive Castro. 'I would hug him and I would say, "God bless you,"' she said. 'I did not hate him. I forgave him years ago. I said, "I forgive whoever done it, just let her go."'

Nancy Ruiz and Ariel Castro had known each other for years. They grew up in the same neighbourhood; her sister lived just two-and-a-half blocks from the house where Gina was held captive and Ruiz walked passed his house regularly. When they bumped into each other, he would offer his support and ask how she was getting on without Gina, when all the time he was imprisoning and abusing her. But even this betrayal was not enough to make Nancy Ruiz hate him. 'When you start to hate a person, that eats you up,' she said. 'I don't have time for that. I have to be, you know, I want to be happy, like I am now.'

Others were not so forgiving. 'I wouldn't be able to look at him,' said Castro's cousin, Maria Castro Montes. 'I couldn't say anything to him. Why? Shame on you? How could you do this? I don't even want to ask him those questions. I don't even want to look at him.'

After nine years of hell, Gina could barely recognize her own home. 'She asked for a tour,' her aunt, Sandra Ruiz, said. 'She was happy.'

The next day, Cleveland residents celebrated the women's rescue, gathering in an open field to release balloons. Those attended said they especially wanted to honour Michelle Knight whose disappearance had not attracted as much publicity as the other two. 'It's in support of her,' said organizer Loretta Freeman.

As the crowd formed a circle and readied themselves to release the balloons, Michelle's grandmother Deborah, who lived only a few miles away from Seymour Avenue, spoke through tears from the centre of the crowd. 'I'm over-whelmed,' she said. 'I want to hug and keep her close to me.' However, she had not yet seen Michelle since she had been rescued from Castro's house and could not comment further. She had been relying on media reports to find out the latest on her granddaughter's situation. 'I've been trying since day one to see her,' she said. 'Amanda Berry and Gina DeJesus have been reunited with their family. We are just sitting here waiting. We are trying to get in touch with her. She has no one there for her right now. We need to get all the family together.'

Deborah's granddaughter Tiffani White was also there and said she felt for the plight of her cousin, who must have thought she had been abandoned. 'There was no one looking for her when she disappeared,' she said. 'I want her to know that there is someone there for her. To find out she was in a basement is devastating ... I have gone through hell and high water to come here to see her. It doesn't seem like she has support, but she does. We just want to hear from her mouth that she is OK. We want her home.'

While Amanda and Gina DeJesus had emotional reunions with their families, Michelle did not. Her mother had flown to Cleveland from her new home in Naples, Florida, in the hope of being reunited with her daughter. She went to the hospital where Michelle was recuperating. Barbara had brought her ten-year-old daughter Katie to Cleveland as well so that she could meet her sister for the first time. But after a week, she had to send Katie back to Naples so she could return to school. It was reported that Michelle's twin brother Freddie was allowed a visit.

The family friend told *MailOnline*, 'All Barbara wants is to see Michelle.'

The following day, a statement was posted to the hospital's Facebook and Twitter accounts, saying that Michelle was 'in good spirits and would like the community to know that she is extremely grateful for the outpouring of flowers and gifts'. She was released later that day and was taken to an unknown destination.

Barbara Knight told NBC's *Today* show, 'I know she's probably angry at the world because she probably thought she'd never be found.' She also said that she hoped the tension that existed between them in the past could be healed, and she wanted to take her daughter back to Florida, where she had moved to after Michelle's disappearance.

But Michelle had been through a lot. Before being abducted, she had been forced to give up her own child; then she had been held captive for almost eleven years, and repeatedly beaten and raped. During her ordeal, she fell pregnant several times but miscarried after being beaten and starved. She was also forced to deliver Castro's daughter by Amanda Berry.

Later, the Cleveland Police posted a handwritten note from her on their Facebook page. Headed, 'This is a special thank you note from a strong and resilient woman who will forever be held dearly in the hearts of the police officers and residents of the 2nd District', it said:

Dear Commander Suizer, officers and staff,
You don't know how much I appreciate all your time and work collecting cards and gifts from people for me and the other girls. I am overwhelmed by the amount of thoughts, love and prayers expressed by complete strangers. It is comforting. Life is tough, but I'm tougher! Just when the

caterpillar thought the world was over, she became a butterfly.

Thanks! God bless you,
Michelle Knight

Barbara turned down several big money offers from TV networks to talk about her daughter.

In the YouTube video the three girls released through a Cleveland-based PR firm on 9 July to thank family and supporters, Michelle said she was building a 'brand-new life'. Reading from a prepared script, she said in a halting voice, 'I may have been through hell and back, but I am strong enough to walk through hell with a smile on my face and my head held high, and my feet firmly on the ground. I will not let the situation define who I am; I will define the situation. I don't want to be consumed by hatred.' She said she had been strong enough to survive and was looking forward to her new life.

Kathy Joseph, Michelle's attorney, said in a statement that the three women wanted 'to say thank you to people from Cleveland and across the world'. Gina DeJesus also thanked the viewers for their support, while Amanda Berry said, 'I want to thank everyone who has helped me and my family through this entire ordeal, everyone who had been there to support us. It has been a blessing to have such an outpouring of love and kindness.' She added, 'I'm getting stronger each day and having my privacy has helped immensely. I ask that everyone continues to respect our privacy and give us time to have a normal life.'

A week after her release, Amanda visited her mother's

grave. Looking to the future, her uncle, 50-year-old Curtis Berry, invited his niece and her daughter to come and live in Elizabethton, Tennessee, where, he said, her family would welcome her with open arms. Amanda's father lived in the rural Tennessee town and she often visited there before being abducted. 'She has more kin here than anywhere else,' said Curtis. 'This is her home.'

Meanwhile, Charles Ramsey's 15 minutes of fame was immortalized when tattoo artist Rodney Rose at 252 Tattoo tattooed his picture on the leg of fellow artist Stephen Munhollon. Normally, it would have cost $700, but Rose did it for free. It took five hours.

'Throughout this whole crazy week we've had in Cleveland, he's kind of been the face and voice of the city,' Rose said of Ramsey. 'He did a great job of representing the city, saying he didn't want the reward money, to give it to the women, and he also brought humour to a dark situation. He's an average guy who stepped up to the plate when he needed to ... and you gotta respect that.' His portrait now nestles between two other tattoos in the back of Munhollon's right calf. Munhollon has more than fifty tattoos, but the other person's face inked on his body is that of Chuck Norris – and his Ramsey tattoo was getting more attention. Munhollon said he was stopped by a group of Cleveland cops so they could take pictures of the tattoo. 'It's a little sore, but it looks fantastic,' Munhollon told the *New York Daily News*.

Ramsey's picture also adorned the front of a T-shirt, along with the legend, 'Cleveland's Hero – Charles Ramsey.' The Facebook page of the restaurant where he worked as a 'dish technician' stated, 'We're extremely proud of our employee

Charles Ramsey for not turning his back on the young women. He's a true Cleveland hero.'

His boss Chris Hodgson told the Cleveland *Plain Dealer*, 'What you see in the video is what you get with Chuck. He's calm in the face of crazy and hectic things going on ... I can't say enough about Chuck. He faced a situation and didn't turn his back on it.'

Not only was he an 'absolute hero', he was a 'phenomenal worker'. 'He was one of those guys who was always willing to pitch in and help, so the fact that he did something like this doesn't surprise me,' said Peter D'Amato, the manager of another restaurant where Ramsey worked.

The self-effacing Ramsey told CNN's Anderson Cooper, 'You gotta' have some cojones, bro. That's all it's about. It's about cojones on this planet.'

Ramsey publicly refused the reward the FBI offered for the return of the women. He said he did not want the money because he already had a job and the women he rescued deserved the money more than he did. 'I'll tell you what you do – give it to them,' Ramsey said.

But Ramsey did get a reward of sorts. Before he became a national hero, he was known locally for his love of barbecues. Supporters started a Rally.org fundraiser to buy him a $5,300 high-end grill and a three-year membership to the 'Sirloin of the Month Club'.

While Ramsey was trending on Twitter, he said he did not seek fame. He merely identified himself as an American, a Christian and a human being. 'I'm just like you. I work for a living,' he said. 'There was a woman in distress. So why turn your back on that? My father would've whooped the hell out of me if had found out that I cowered out.'

But Ramsey was no saint. In the early 1990s, he had convictions for drug abuse, criminal trespass and receiving stolen goods. And the 43-year-old was busted three times for domestic abuse between 1997 and 2003. 'Those incidents helped me become the man I am today and are the reason why I try to help the community as much as I can ... including those women,' he said.

But the past would not be forgotten by some. It was reported that the 6ft 2in, 16½st Ramsey assaulted his then-wife Rochelle, who claimed he was now failing to pay his $51-a-month child support for their 15-year-old daughter. In August 1998, after his prior domestic violence cases had been consolidated, Ramsey was sentenced to six months in jail, plus five years' probation and counselling. But he was arrested again for domestic violence in January 2003. This time, he was indicted for a felony because of his prior convictions and, while Ramsey was in state prison, his wife filed for divorce, ending their eight-year marriage.

But Ramsey said he shouldn't be pilloried for his past. 'If I had so much hatred for women, I would have minded my own business this week and walked away instead of risking my life to save someone else,' he said.

Meanwhile, Angelo Cordero challenged Ramsey's right to wear the hero's laurels. He claimed that it was he, not Charles Ramsey, who first helped Amanda Berry break out of the house where she was being held captive. 'I helped her and I was first,' Cordero told a reporter from the local NewsChannel5 in Spanish. 'Ramsey arrived after she was outside with the girl. But the truth who arrived there, who crossed the street, who came and broke the door, it was me.'

Cordero and Anna Tejeda's husband Wintel, who was also

on hand at the rescue, said they were not jealous of the attention Ramsey has received. 'I did what had to be done. I helped her,' Cordero said. 'They have their daughter; daughters are safe over there.'

Even so, it was Ramsey who was afforded the red-carpet treatment. Internet users auto-tuned his TV interviews on YouTube and racked up more than 16 million hits. For mentioning that he was eating a Big Mac at the time of the rescue in his interviews, McDonald's used Twitter to applaud his efforts and the fast-food chain promised to be in touch.

Even Rochelle came to his defence, posting old photos of Ramsey on Facebook. 'OK, for the record, people do change and you shouldn't hold the past against someone,' she wrote. 'The thing is Charles Ramsey did a good deed and those girls are safe ... is that not the most important thing?'

Ramsey picked up some $15,000 in speaking fees. He also launched a personal website where he sells T-shirts bearing his image for $25, and digital downloads of the song 'Dead Giveaway', which used clips from his 911 call and became a viral sensation. He paid off his debts and bought a second-hand BMW for $8,000.

Soon after the story first broke, Ramsey moved out of the area and into a small hotel room outside Cleveland. Since then, he said, no fewer than a dozen landlords have denied his rental applications for fear of the attention he attracts. As a result, he became homeless and was sleeping in his car. Rescuing Castro's captives, Ramsey said, had ruined his life. 'I don't have an address, I don't live anywhere. I go from house to house, friend to friend, family member to family member,' he told the *Daily Mail*. 'What I've been doing for the past four weeks is wearing out my welcome with everybody who knows me.'

Since the kidnap story had broken, he also lost his job and could not find a new one because employers were wary of the public interest in him. And fame brought him other unwanted headaches. He said he tried to shut down a counterfeit Facebook page and had unsuccessfully attempted to stop a Chinese company from selling a video game that uses his image as a character. 'I'm borrowing money from my relatives,' he said. Meanwhile, he did not dare answer his phone because creditors kept calling.

Nevertheless, he told the *Daily Mail* he would not trade in his notoriety, despite all the problems it had caused him. 'Would you go back to not being famous? Yes or no?' he said rhetorically. 'Of course not, no you wouldn't, so going back as far as me being famous, of course I'm not gonna give that up.'

While Charles Ramsey was paying the price of fame, Castro's house at 2207 Seymour Avenue became a tourist destination. Although the Cleveland Police had boarded up the windows and erected a tall fence around the building, people were flocking to see the place where Castro had imprisoned and abused his captives. 'It's like they got a movie or something over there,' said one neighbour. 'A lot of people are going to come from other states to take a picture of the house.'

The police guarded the house 24 hours a day due to arson threats. 'It's still a crime scene,' Sergeant Sam Morris told the *New York Daily News*. 'We're protecting the integrity of it.'

But that did not stop curious visitors from taking a look. Stan Miller travelled from ten miles away just to see the house. 'I just came to see it with my own eyes, but next time I come, I'll probably bring my cell phone, take a picture,' Miller told local TV station WKYC.

The media were also interested. A photograph of the piles of junk, barbed wire and chains in the backyard snapped by a neighbour appeared on CNN. Among the debris there was a new Barbie bike for Jocelyn and, mounted above the back door, was a car wing mirror so Castro could see who was there.

With just ten days to go until the trial, the FBI obtained a new search warrant for Castro's home and sent in a team to collect soil samples. They did not say what they were looking for.

While the initial reports of the women's health were upbeat, it later leaked that they may require long-term therapy for hearing loss and joint and muscle damage due to the maltreatment. In the basement, the women had been either chained to the wall, or held on dog leashes attached to the ceiling. They were bound with duct tape and kept in stress positions for long periods that left them with bed sores and other injuries.

Amanda Berry was treated better that the other two and, when they were released, she took the glare of the media spotlight, while Michelle Knight remained behind closed doors and Gina DeJesus appeared under a hoodie. 'One of the girls has difficulty moving her head around from being chained up,' an anonymous source told the *New York Daily News*. The victim was identified as Gina DeJesus. 'It was like they were POWs. They had bed sores from being left in positions for extended lengths of time,' the source said.

When not chained up in the basement, the girls were

confined to the bedrooms that were only furnished with a mattress on the floor. All the bedroom doors in the house had padlocks on the outside and their movement around the house was very restricted.

If Castro left the house for an extended period he would cover their faces, including their eyes, with duct tape, leaving only a small opening so they could breathe. When he returned, he would rip the duct tape off, taking with it hair and skin.

Michelle Knight was particularly badly treated. A police report said she was starved for weeks on end, raped repeatedly and punched in the stomach to induce miscarriages, resulting in charges of foetal homicide.

All three women exhibited signs of malnutrition, but these were particularly acute in Michelle Knight and Gina DeJesus. Castro used food to torment them. He would bring food to one of the girls, leaving the other two to watch her eat. Or he would feed two of them, making the other one watch. Sometimes he alone would eat, leaving all three to starve. But this did not work as well as he thought. As Michelle Knight and Gina DeJesus shared a room, they found ways to sneak food to each other.

It was revealed that Castro usually kept one woman upstairs and the other two – generally Knight and DeJesus – in the basement. The worst treatment, it seems, was meted out to Michelle Knight. A friend of the family told CNN that Castro often hit her with hand weights and other objects, using her as a 'punching bag' for 11 years. However, Michelle issued a statement to CNN saying, 'I am healthy, happy and safe and will reach out to family, friends and supporters in good time.'

Quoting police sources, the *National Enquirer* said that Castro had no interest in having children with Knight, because she was only 4ft 7in and he believed her to be 'mentally disabled'. The paper also said that Castro was grooming his six-year-old daughter to be another sex slave because the other captives 'were getting to old for him'.

Terri Weaver, a professor of psychology at the St Louis University, said that the girls would have been helped by each other's presence. 'Having someone who has been a witness to those intimate details can really forge a powerful bond because there is a shared understanding,' she said. This bond may well have been strengthened by the birth of Jocelyn during their captivity. It was unclear, though, whether that bond would be maintained after they were freed, Professor Weaver said. Some people who have shared traumatic experiences seek to maintain that bond, while others seek to put the experience behind them.

When they were discovered, it was said that the women were in a worse condition than the dogs Castro kept. Two terrier-poodle mixes were found in the house, and there was a Chihuahua in the car with Castro the night he was arrested. The role of the dogs is unclear. There was some talk in law-enforcement circles that the dogs were pets for the women. The 'R.I.P.' scrawled on the wall of the basement may have referred to a pet. However, some thought that the dogs acted as a 'noise shield' for the captives; any sounds made by the captives and overheard could be ascribed to the animals.

The dogs were not in great condition either. The terrier-poodles had matted hair and needed grooming. All three dogs were taken to animal rescue kennels where they were

THE DISAPPEARED

cleaned up. The FBI asked the dog warden to hold on to them in case any of the victims wanted to adopt them. Otherwise, they would be sent to dog foster homes before being put up for public adoption.

10

GUILTY

O n Friday, 26 July, with just ten days to go before the scheduled start of the trial, Castro suddenly changed his plea. To avoid the death penalty, he pleaded guilty to 937 charges in a deal that would give him life in prison. As a result of the guilty plea, the three victims would not have to testify in court.

The women's law firm, Jones Day, released a statement expressing their relief. It said, 'Amanda, Gina and Michelle are relieved by today's plea. They are satisfied by this resolution to the case, and are looking forward to having these legal proceedings draw to a final close in the near future. They do not wish to speak to the media or anyone else, and they thank people for continuing to respect their privacy as they grow stronger.'

Again, Castro appeared before Judge Michael Russon at Cuyahoga County Common Pleas. He wore an orange prison jumpsuit, a full beard and glasses, and still had his wrists handcuffed in front of him. For the first time, he appeared awake and attentive. The judge asked him if he had received his glasses and whether they were OK. Looking up at the judge, Castro replied, 'Yes it is, Your Honour, thank you.'

The judge asked Castro whether he had read the plea agreement, discussed it with his lawyers, was aware of its contents and consented to its terms.

'I am fully aware and I do consent to it,' he replied.

He was then asked whether he understood that there would be no trial and he answered, 'I am aware of it.'

The judge repeatedly told him that he would never be freed from jail and asked, 'Is that clear?'

'I do understand that, Your Honour,' Castro replied.

The prosecution also made it clear that he would never even get a parole hearing in Ohio. Then the judge went through the charges and, over and over, Castro repeated one word – 'Guilty.'

In previous hearings, Castro had kept his head bowed and his eyes closed; this time his head was held high. Asked how good his English was, Castro replied that his reading and spelling were good, but 'there are some things I do not comprehend because of my sexual problems throughout the years,' he said. 'But I trust my lawyers and I understand my rights and the sentence.' He even sought to mitigate his crimes.

'My addiction to pornography and sexual problems in general has taken a toll on my mind,' he said. 'I would like to state I was a victim as a child and it just kept going.'

The judge cut him off, telling him to save the story for his sentencing hearing when his victims would also have a chance to speak. The judge then told him that he would be classified as a sexually violent predator. Castro said he understood this, but disagreed with the classification, saying that he was not violent. 'The violent part I don't agree on,' he said.

In another jarring moment, he said of the child whom he had fathered by rape, 'I would just like to state I miss my daughter very much.'

It was also pointed out that, since his arrest, he had co-operated with the authorities. 'I said I was willing to work with the FBI and I would tell them everything,' he told the court.

Asked whether he understood that he would die in prison, he said, 'I do understand that and I said because of the sex crimes I knew I was pretty much going to get the book thrown at me.'

The prosecutors said that, if evidence of other crimes came to light, Castro could still be indicted to charges that may invite the death penalty. Meanwhile, it was announced that his house would be torn down. His other property and assets were forfeit.

McGinty said that experts would be called to discuss how significant a part Stockholm Syndrome had played in the victims' failure to escape earlier. The syndrome is a psychological response often seen in people taken hostage, where the victim shows signs of loyalty to the hostage-taker, regardless of what they have suffered or the danger the hostage has faced. There are reports that hostages have even fallen in love with their captors.

The syndrome was first identified after a robbery at the

Norrmalmstorg branch of Kreditbanken in Stockholm in 1973, where bank employees were held hostage from 23 to 28 August. It was noted the victims had become strongly emotionally attached to their captors, and even defended them after they were freed from their six-day ordeal. The term 'Stockholm Syndrome' was coined by the criminologist and psychiatrist Nils Bejerot, who assisted the police during the robbery. Famous cases include that of Patty Hearst, the heiress to the US newspaper empire of William Randolph Hearst who was kidnapped in 1974 by left-wing radicals calling themselves the Symbionese Liberation Army. After two months in captivity, she was filmed taking part in a robbery with her captors and issued statements condemning the capitalist 'crimes' of her parents, using the name 'Tania' – the *nom de guerre* of Tamara Bunka, the comrade-in-arms and lover of Argentine revolutionary Che Guevara. The rest of the SLA were killed in a shoot-out in May 1974, but Patty Hearst remained at large until September 1975, when she was captured by the FBI. She was charged with bank robbery and firearms offences. In her defence, she claimed that she had suffered from Stockholm Syndrome and had been coerced into aiding the SLA. She was convicted and imprisoned for her actions in the robbery, although her sentence was commuted in February 1979 by President Jimmy Carter, and she later received a Presidential pardon from Bill Clinton.

On the day they were rescued, Michelle Knight and Gina DeJesus were initially afraid to show themselves even when five police officers had entered the house, prosecutor McGinty said. When they overcame their fear, they clung to police so tightly the officers could not use their flashlights. 'That told me what fear this man put into these women and how much courage it took to survive this ordeal,' McGinty said. He also spoke of the 'mental and physical bond and barrier' that the first woman who escaped, Amanda Berry, had the courage to overcome.

On the day after Castro pleaded guilty, Amanda Berry made a surprise appearance on stage at a music festival with rapper Nelly. Wearing sunglasses, jeans and a black T-shirt, she walked on stage at the Roverfest concert in Cleveland that Saturday night with her sister and a friend. The announcer called for a round of applause and a cheer bigger than for any of the acts that had played that night. She smiled broadly while waving and acknowledging the applause, but she did not address the crowd. Then the DJ said, 'I told her she had a little bit of time to make up on the partying and you guys could help her out tonight.' She held hands with one of the men who appeared on stage with her and he draped a protective arm around her throughout her appearance, while the audience chanted her name.

Nelly called Amanda back to the stage after his music set and, calling for more applause, said, 'Everyone, here's Amanda Berry.'

'I just wanted Cleveland to know that we were proud of her,' Nelly told MTV News.

Concertgoer Kayleigh Fladung told the *Plain Dealer*, 'She didn't say anything, but she was smiling and happy. She waved to the crowd, everyone went crazy cheering, and she went backstage. Nelly did his set – four or five songs – and then he brought her out again and everyone cheered. It was cool to see but still very surprising.'

Shane French, the host of the syndicated talk show *Rover's Morning Glory* on WMMS in Cleveland, had offered her an impromptu invitation over the air, but had no idea that she was listening. 'I just said that she had ten years of partying to make up for and she should come,' French said. He was surprised when security guards told him Amanda had arrived, having no idea that she would take him up on his offer. At first, Amanda refused to go on stage, but then agreed if French would go with her.

'She didn't say why she decided to come, but some of her family members told me they listen to my show every day and had been to Roverfest in the past,' French said.

Overcome by the crowd's cheers, Amanda cried, according to the women with her. 'I didn't see her cry, but I think she was pretty overwhelmed by the response that the crowd gave her,' said French. 'She just seemed to be having a great time.' However, French had not invited her to appear on his radio show. 'I figured that when she wants to tell her story, she'll make the arrangements, and it would have been pointless to even ask,' he said.

Gina DeJesus's mother Nancy Ruiz was pleased for Amanda. She told NewsChannel 5, 'I am excited for her. I am so proud of her. I'm glad that she's out and about, and this is what these girls need.' But Gina was not yet ready to face the public and volunteers erected a $3,000, 6ft privacy fence so she could sunbathe in her mother's garden in seclusion.

In the aftermath of the Cleveland kidnappings, crimes against women did not abate in Cleveland as abandoned homes were being searched for the bodies of victims of a new serial killer. Three bodies were found on 20 July. One was found in a field, wrapped in trash bags; another was dumped in a garage; and the third was in the basement of an empty house in a dilapidated part of Cleveland.

The first to be identified was that of 38-year-old Angela Deskins. Her family said she was a 'wonderful daughter, sister and aunt who truly cared about her family and friends'. She was naked and her body showed signs of trauma.

The father of 18-year-old Shirellda Helen Terry was out handing out flyers in the hope of finding his daughter when he was told that she had been identified as the second victim. 'The tears have poured, the pain is there and it's final – right now we just got to move to the next step,' her father Van Terry told ABC5. His daughter was last seen at 1.30pm on 10 July as she walked home from her summer job at an elementary school.

Shirellda's grandmother, Rosetta Terry, had also been helping to hand out flyers when Mr Terry broke the news to her. 'She was a good girl; she was a hugger,' Mrs Terry said. 'We used to tease her that we were gonna put her on a hug diet.'

Shirellda was a caring teenager who attended Bible study groups and who would frequently call and send texts to her mother.

The third victim, 28-year-old Shetisha Sheeley, was identified by her tattoos and fingerprints. She had been arrested in June 2012, charged with firing a weapon from a vehicle, but the case was later dismissed. According to her court-appointed attorney, Michael Nelson, no witnesses saw her discharging the weapon. She had come from a troubled family background, and her 25-year-old brother Dontel had been shot dead the previous December in an unrelated incident. Her mother feared the worst when Shetisha failed to turn up for his funeral.

'She lived on the edge,' Mr Nelson said. 'The streets are just mean. She was a vulnerable person, and with that it probably multiplied her risk.' Her 12-year-old daughter lived with relatives.

It was thought that they were all killed by the same person. 'One of the things that makes us believe it's the same suspect is the way that they were all wrapped ... and the same concealment of each of the victims,' said East Cleveland Mayor Gary Norton. 'We are dealing with a sick individual, and we have reason to believe that there might be more victims.'

Thirty-five-year-old registered sex offender Michael Manson has been charged with their murder. Mayor Norton said that, during police questioning, Madison had revealed that Anthony Sowell might have inspired the killings. 'He said some things that led us to believe that in some way, shape or form, Sowell might be an influence,' Mayor Norton told the wire service Associated Press. Meanwhile, the police, city employees and volunteers continued the search for more bodies.

Ariel Castro appeared in court one last time on 1 August 2013 for sentencing. He was brought in at 9.00am, again wearing an orange prison jumpsuit. The first witness was Officer Barbara Johnson, who was one of the first to arrive at what they were now calling the Cleveland House of Horrors on Seymour Avenue. The girls, she said, were very pale, very thin and very scared when the police found them. 'Michelle Knight literally launched herself at another

officer and kept repeating, "You saved us ... you saved us,"'
she said.

Dr Gerald Maloney, who was on duty in the emergency
room when the three victims arrived in hospital, said that
they were 'very much emotionally fragile at the time'.
They were emotionally distraught and said they had been
held against their will and sexually assaulted. Michelle
Knight, particularly, was bruised and emaciated. He said
she requested that no male physicians treat her. Other
witnesses described the women as malnourished, pale and
traumatized.

There was a cutaway model of Castro's house in the court
and pictures of the interior were produced while Detective
Harasimchuk described how the victims were chained up in
the basement and raped. He said that Castro would put a
motorbike helmet on each girl and left them in the dark
basement overnight.

All three had been abducted after accepting a lift from
Castro, only to find themselves chained in his basement
and raped within a few hours of being kidnapped.

'Each woman told me they were repeatedly sexually,
physically and emotionally abused by Ariel Castro during
the entire time they were in captivity,' he said.

All three had been repeatedly raped vaginally, orally and
anally throughout their imprisonment.

Dr Frank Ochberg, professor of clinical psychiatry at
Michigan State University, described the victims as having
suffered prolonged 'terror-induced states of mind,
defilement, dehumanization and ... they were treated like
animals and deprived of their sense of self and dignity'.
Outlining the long-term impact of a decade of continuous

abuse, he said, 'They have life sentences. They will never be free of the damage done.'

The memories of their captivity would not go away as they had been abducted at an age when humans learn to be intimate. But what they got from Castro was something entirely different. 'This was not real intimacy,' Ochberg said. 'This was a perversion of intimacy.' He went on to describe the women's survival and coping skills as 'marvellous, compelling examples of resilience, of imagination, of humanity'.

In his evaluation, he said that Castro 'appeared to be evolving in an ever more dangerous direction, capturing younger and younger women, telling his captives he was hunting for replacements. These and other threats had the effect of terrifying the victims into subservience.' He added, 'Castro hurt each of the three young women that he captured and confined in ways that create lasting wounds. He terrified them. The body responds to terror long afterward with uncontrollable visions, smells, sounds and sensations. These are called trauma memories and they are unlike ordinary memory. They come at night in the form of nightmares.'

Michelle Knight, he said, had suffered 'the longest and most severely'. Castro had admitted that on one occasion Michelle had told him she may be pregnant and he forced a termination by putting her on a tea-only diet and made her perform jumping jacks and 'knee bends'.

When Amanda Berry was in labour, Dr Ochberg said, 'It was Michelle who served as doctor, nurse, midwife and paediatrician during the birth. She breathed life into that infant when she wasn't breathing ... At other times, she interceded when Castro sought to abuse Gina, interposing herself and absorbing physical and sexual trauma. But each survivor had a will to prevail and used that will to live through the ordeal.'

An expert on Stockholm Syndrome and traumatic memories, Dr Ochberg made his evaluation of the women after viewing police interviews on video and checking medical records and FBI reports. He said the women 'managed to share faith and friendship' on the rare occasions they were allowed to be together. As a unit, they home-schooled Amanda Berry's baby and instilled 'honourable values' when they could. 'This is the good news,' he said. 'But it does not in any way paint a rosy picture for normalcy or a quick recovery. Grave damage has been done.'

Forensic psychologist Dr Gregory Saathoff described the women's ordeal as a 'complete and comprehensive captivity' and said when he first learned of Castro's crimes, he noted, 'The scope and magnitude of Ariel Castro's crimes is unprecedented.' Asked if Castro suffered from mental illness, Saathoff said that his examination showed Castro suffered from 'no psychiatric illness whatsoever'.

The court was also told how Castro controlled the movements of the women by keeping them in locked rooms and tying or chaining them up. 'There is only one bathroom in the house, on the first floor,' a report said. 'The defendant would not allow the victims downstairs to use the bathroom. They only had access to plastic toilets in the bedrooms. They were emptied infrequently ... He controlled the temperature and the inflow of food and drink. He used the cold of the basement and the heat of the attic as punishment techniques.'

THE DISAPPEARED

FBI agent Andrew Burke described the moment when he first met the victims who were pale and malnourished. 'I'll never forget it,' he said. 'It was surreal to me. I had been involved in the missing-persons investigations for quite some time.'

Burke talked the court through a series of pictures of the inside of Castro's house. The back door was equipped with an alarm, while a hanging bedspread then separated the living area from the kitchen. A porch swing obstructed access to stairs, then a curtain closed off the upstairs area where the women were imprisoned.

Castro had built a virtual prison inside his ramshackle home with a makeshift alarm system and the girls were chained up behind the bolted doors of their bedrooms. The house was divided up in such a way as to make it more secure and conceal the rooms where the women were held. The bedroom windows were boarded up from the inside with heavy closet doors. The doorknobs had been removed from the bedroom doors and replaced with numerous locks. Holes the size of saucers were cut in the outer doors to help air circulate. The pictures of dirty mattresses draped in chains were from the room where Michelle Knight and Gina DeJesus were kept, Burke explained. Several pairs of manacles were also found in the house.

A large amount of cash was found in a washing machine in the basement. This was next to the pole the women were chained to when Castro raped them. After he had sexually abused them, he would throw money at them, as if paying a prostitute. Then he would take the money back to buy any items they wanted when he left the house. In another bizarre game, he would force them to hold a gun to his head and dare them to shoot him.

Castro's handwritten suicide note was shown to the court. It was headed, 'Confession and Details'. In it, Castro described the terrible things he forced the women to undergo while in captivity. 'Bottom line, I am a sexual predator,' it said.

Cuyahoga County Sheriff's Detective Dave Jacobs said that Castro had also confessed to him when they talked a few days after he had been arrested. According to Jacobs, Castro had said, 'I knew what I did was wrong.' Castro then tried to apologize to the victims, but Judge Michael Russo said he could do that later in the proceedings.

Of the victims, only Michelle Knight appeared in court to give a victim impact statement. It was her first public appearance since she had been released from Castro's home. 'You took eleven years of my life away and I have got it back,' she told Castro. 'I spent eleven years in hell; now your hell is just beginning. You will face hell for eternity. From this moment on, I will not let you define me, or affect who I am. I will live on, you will die a little each day as you think about the eleven years and atrocities you inflicted on us. I know there's a lot of people going through hard times but they need someone to reach out a hand for them to hold and let them know they are being heard.'

She condemned his hypocrisy – he went to church every Sunday, then came home to rape and torture them. 'I remember all the times you came home talking about what everyone else was doing wrong when you were doing the same thing,' she said. 'You said, "At least I didn't kill you." You took eleven years from my life, but I've got my life back.'

Through her tears she added, 'I missed my son every day. I wondered if I was ever going to see him again. He was only two-and-a-half when I was taken. I would look inside my heart and see my son. I cried every night ... I was so alone. I worried what would happen to me and the other girls every day. Days never got shorter. Days turned into nights, nights turned into days. The years turned into eternity. I knew nobody cared about me. He told me that my family didn't care. Nobody should ever have to go through what I went through ... Christmas was a most traumatic day because I didn't get to spend it with my son.'

She also spoke of her 'team-mate' Gina, saying, 'Gina and I were a team. She never let me fall ... I never let her fall. She nursed me back to health when I was dying from his abuse. My friendship with her is the only good thing to come out of this situation. We said that we would someday make it out alive and we did.'

Addressing Castro directly, she said, 'I will overcome all this that happened. I will live on; you will die a little every day. I will forgive you, but I will never forget. With God's guidance, I'll prevail and help other victims who may have suffered at the hands of another.'

Michelle also expressed her satisfaction in the sentence. 'The death penalty will be the easy way out,' she said. 'You don't deserve that. We want you to spend the rest of your life in prison.'

Representing the DeJesus family, Gina's cousin Sylvia Colon said, 'Today is the last day we want to think or talk about this; we will continue to live and love. It is not for us to judge or determine any punishment. Only a higher power can do that.'

Then she talked of her cousin Gina. 'She thrives, she laughs, she swims, she dances, she loves and she is loved. She will finish school, go to college, fall in love and – if she chooses – get married and have children. She lives not as a victim, but a survivor.' Then she turned to Castro and said, in Spanish, 'May God have mercy on your soul.'

Amanda Berry's sister Beth Serrano cried as she read a statement. She told the court that Amanda did not want to talk about what happened for the sake of her child.

'Amanda is not here today. She is strong and beautiful, inside and out ... she's not only my sister, she's the best friend I have, the best person I know. She does not want to talk about this day or be forced to talk about it. She would love to be the person who decides when and how to tell her daughter. Her concern is that her daughter will read about things said by people at the wrong time. Please continue to respect her privacy ... she does not want other people to talk or write about it. For such a long time, she had no control over her life ... please let her have control over this so she can protect her daughter.'

Finally, Castro was given a chance to tell his side of the story. Although he had pleaded guilty, Castro was unrepentant. In a long and rambling statement, he tried to justify his heinous crimes, depicting himself as a person who had 'everything going for him' who was brought down by an addiction to porn. 'I believe I am addicted to porn to the point that it really makes me impulsive and I just don't realize what I'm doing is wrong,' he said. He tried to blame his job which was stressful, sexual problems, his history of abuse, even his wife. 'They're trying to say that I'm a violent person,' he said. 'I am not a violent person – I am a happy person inside. I drove a school bus, I was a musician, I have a family. I do have value for human life because every time I came home, I would be so glad for the situation, as crazy as it sounds.'

He complained that people were trying to portray him as a monster and denied that he would return home to beat the girls. 'I'm not a monster,' he said. 'I'm a normal person. I'm sick ... I have an addiction, just like an alcoholic has an addiction ... I did not prey on these women. I just acted on my sexual instincts.' The former bandsman continued, 'To be a musician and to be a monster like you're trying to say that I am – I don't think I can handle that – I'm a happy person inside.' He said he never planned to abduct the women, but acted on the spur of the moment when he kidnapped his first victim and told the court that he had been 'driven by sex'.

Despite pleading guilty on 937 counts, he denied ever beating the girls, raping them or torturing them. 'As God is my witness, I never beat these women like they are trying to say ... I never tortured them,' he said. 'These women were not virgins when I met them, all three of them. The sex inside the house was consensual ... I did not force sex on them.' He even blamed the FBI. They had let the girls down by not questioning him properly and he claimed that the girls were happy in captivity.

'I'm not sure there's anyone in America that would agree with you,' Judge Michael Russo interjected.

Again Castro insisted, 'All the sex was consensual. The girls were not virgins. They had multiple sex partners before me.' Showing not a flicker of remorse, he went on, 'We had a lot of harmony that went on in that home. I am not a violent predator. I simply kept them there so they couldn't leave. Amanda, she got in my vehicle without knowing who it was. I'm not trying to put the fault on her, but I'm just trying to make a point across I'm not a violent predator ... I just wanted to clear the record that I'm not a monster.'

Castro then referred to Amanda's recent appearance at the Roverfest concert. 'That right there itself proves that girl did not go through no torture,' he insisted. 'If that was true, do you think she would be out there partying already and having fun? I don't think so.' Again, he claimed the sex that took place inside the house was consensual. The girls, he said, would even ask him for sex. 'These allegations about being forceful upon them, that is totally wrong,' he said.

However, he broke down in tears when he talked about Jocelyn and admitted that he should have taken her to hospital for treatment. But his sex addiction had reached a point where he had to 'practise the art of masturbation and pornography' two to three hours a day.

He became argumentative over the aggravated murder charge, saying that there was no evidence that his abuse had aborted Michelle Knight's pregnancy. Judge Russo reminded him that he had pleaded guilty to this charge. Castro shot back that he had only done that to save the victims more trauma. He also objected to being called a 'violent sexual predator'. Judge Russo pointed out that he had admitted this by 'virtue of your plea'.

Castro concluded with an apology. 'Finally,' he said, 'I would like to apologize to the victims – to Amanda Berry, Gina DeJesus and Michelle Knight. I am truly sorry for what happened. To this day, I'm trying to answer my own questions. I don't know why. A man that had everything going on for himself – I had a job, I had a home, I had vehicles, I had my musical talent. I had everything going on for me.'

Turning to Michelle Knight and the families of the other victims, he said, 'I am truly sorry. Thank you, victims. Please find it in your heart to forgive me.'

Judge Russo then formally sentenced him to life in prison without parole plus 1,000 years, telling Castro there was no room in society for people who enslave others. 'There is no place in this city, country or world for those who enslave or brutalize others,' he said. 'You preyed on three young women and subjected them to insurmountable torture. Though they suffered terribly, they did not give up hope. You thought you dominated them, but you didn't. These women never gave up hope. In fact, they prevailed.'

Judge Russo said that Castro suffered 'extreme narcissism' and told him that he would die behind bars. 'A person can only die in prison once,' he said, but the sentence of life without parole plus 1,000 years was 'commensurate with the harm you have done'. 'You don't deserve to be out in our community. You're too dangerous,' he said. Russo told Castro that he 'will never be released from incarceration during the period of his remaining natural life for any reason'.

Then Castro was led away. Knight looked on smiling.

While Castro was taken into solitary confinement to protect him from other prisoners, Michelle Knight, Amanda Berry and Gina DeJesus returned to the House of Horrors which, they said, no longer frightens them. They wanted to thank the neighbours who had helped in their rescue.

Later, Castro's son Anthony went on TV to say that his father's sentence was fully justified. 'I think it's the best possible sentence,' he said. 'I think if he really can't control his impulses and he really doesn't have any value for human life the way this case has shown, then behind bars is where he belongs for the rest of his life.' He vowed never to visit him. 'I was shocked because of the magnitude of such a crime,' he said. 'I don't think I could ever imagine anyone doing that, let alone to find out it was my own flesh and blood, my father.'

He, too, was abused by his father as a child. 'I remember crying myself to sleep when I was a kid because my legs were covered in welts from belts,' he said. 'Seeing my mom get beat up in our own home – no one should ever have to see their mom crumpled up in the corner on the floor so many times.'

Anthony Castro was also pleased that his father did not get the death penalty, but only because it would have brought his punishment to a swift conclusion. 'It's been a three-month nightmare,' he said, 'nothing compared with what the girls went through, but this has been incredibly hard.'

Michelle Knight turned up in Seymour Avenue on 7 August 2013 to watch Castro's house being demolished. After making a brief statement, she released balloons into the air as a symbol of freedom. 'Nobody was there for me when I was missing,' she said. 'And I want the people out there to know, including the mothers, that they can have strength, they can have hope, and their child will come back, they will.' She told the TV cameras, 'I feel very liberated that people think of me as a hero and a role model … and I would love to continue being that.'

Gina DeJesus watched from across the road while one of her aunts, Peggy Arida, was in the cab of the excavator when it struck the first blow against the house. Members of Castro's family, including his son Anthony, had visited earlier that day to pick up personal items including guitars, bicycles and old photographs. Another of the relatives, Gina's aunt, Janice Smith, said that Gina was delighted that the house was being torn down. 'I think it was great for her,' Smith said. 'It was medicine.'

Cuyahoga County Prosecutor Tim McGinty said Castro had cried when he signed over the house deed and mentioned his 'many happy memories' there with the women. This illustrated Castro's 'distorted and twisted' personality, McGinty said.

The two houses to the left of Castro's were also being torn down and the vacant lot was to be developed into a park or whatever local residents decided. Authorities also made sure the rubble did not end up in the wrong hands to be sold on as gruesome memorabilia.

On 4 September 2013, Ariel Castro was found hanged in his cell. Prison staff were unable to revive him. He was later pronounced dead in hospital. The verdict: suicide. It seems that he had inflicted the death sentence upon himself that he had aimed to avoid by pleading guilty.

PART II

MORE MISSING AMERICANS

11

THE HOUSTON HOSTAGES

After the Ohio slave girls had been released, four homeless men were discovered allegedly being held captive in Houston, Texas. The elderly men were found in the garage, while three women were found in the house in front. According to investigators, the conditions they were held in were said to be deplorable and the outer door was nailed shut. All were malnourished and three of them were so weak they could not walk and had to be carried out on a stretcher. They were rushed to Lyndon B Johnson General Hospital.

A neighbour had called 911 to express concern about men in the house in north Houston. When the police arrived, they had to prise open the front door. Inside, they found a trash-filled converted garage. One of the men told officials that he had been there for over ten years.

However, from the outside, the purple-trimmed, one-storey, three-bedroom, brick-built house in Whitecastle

Lane, North Houston, looked normal enough from the outside. It was valued at $55,000. Originally, a non-profit-making charity had been set up there by 57-year-old Regina Jones providing food and shelter for the homeless. Property records showed that the house was owned by Essie Mae Scranton, Regina Jones' 81-year-old mother. There is no suggestion that either woman was involved in any criminal activity arising out of this investigation. Regina's brother Karey Scranton said, 'That's not no shelter. I don't know what my sister did or what she conjured up or whatever.'

'They clearly stated to us they were being held against their will,' Houston Police Department spokeswoman Jodi Silva told the *Houston Chronicle*, adding that the garage had no access to a lavatory and that the men were fed scraps. A bucket or portable toilet may have been provided, the police said.

'One of them seemed to think he was picked up off the street and brought here,' said Sergeant JW McCoy. 'In exchange for beer and cigarettes and a place to stay, he had to turn over his Social Security cheque.'

The four men – ages 79, 74, 65 and 54 – were alleged to have lived in the garage, which had locks on its doors, one chair, no bed or bathroom and a dodgy air conditioner. They slept on a linoleum floor and had no access to a bathroom. Investigators at the scene called their living conditions 'deplorable' and found it difficult to determine how long the men had lived there, although the police said that it was at least one year.

Neighbour Monica Booker said her mother, who also lived in the neighbourhood, told her that she had seen elderly men living there for four years. She also said that three of the women living there were mother, daughter and granddaughter.

She said she had previously spoken to the elderly residents. They appeared to be in good health and none ever told her or anybody she knew that they were being held against their will. Nor had any of them ever asked her for help, she said.

After the men were released, Ms Booker said, 'It's so upsetting,' adding that if she had sensed something was wrong or that the men did not wish to be there, she would have done something to help.

The police said they had been lured there by the promise of food and alcohol, then had been held against their will and forced to hand over their government benefit cheques. They were not shackled or tied up, but there was an elaborate series of locks. The police said the men were given scraps to eat. They were treated for malnutrition and later released and placed in sheltered housing.

In all, there were four women in the house. However, the police said that the women did not appear to have been held captive. Their living conditions were described as more normal.

Court records show 31-year-old Walter Renard Jones was arrested and charged, initially, on two counts of injury to the elderly – that is injury by act and injury by omission – and was held in the Harris County Jail on $200,000 bail. He was listed in state records as one of the directors of Regina's Faith Ministries.

Homicide Sergeant Steve Murdock said that the men said Jones 'used force and coercion to keep them there for the purpose of monetary gain'.

'We're still in the beginning in the investigation,' said Houston Police Department spokeswoman Jodi Silva. 'We still need to determine things like where the money was going.'

Karey Scranton rode to the defence of his nephew. 'The boy would give the shirt off his back to help somebody,' he said. 'He's not no bad person.'

At the hearing, prosecutor Lynne Parsons said Jones was accused of hitting an elderly man with a cane and failing to provide adequate nutrition. Both of these charges were first-degree felonies. 'This particular victim had been invited into the home for coverage, for protection and shelter in exchange for his Social Security cheque,' Parsons said. 'We are continuing the investigation into other allegations about what was going on this house.'

Regina's Faith Ministries had been registered with the state as a non-profit organization in December 2008, although it had been operating before them. Another of the ministries' directors, the pastor of New Rock of Salvation Holiness Church in Houston, Henry Bolden, said he was shocked by what had been going on there.

'I thought they were doing good,' he said. The pastor said he bought ten mattresses for the facility and sometimes would supply it with food, but had little else to do with it. 'I thought they were feeding them pretty good,' he said. 'Maybe I should have checked in there more.'

The Coalition for the Homeless of Houston/Harris County, a non-profit organization that co-ordinates various local efforts, had not heard of this establishment before the four men were discovered, said Marilyn Brown, the group's president and CEO. Brown said some facilities call themselves 'group homes'. However, she said, 'Some of them are more legitimate than others.'

The regulation of such facilities, which provide personal care services such as feeding and dressing, falls to the Texas Department of Ageing and Disability Services. They are required to be state-licensed only if they provide services to four or more individuals. In November 2011 the agency spoke with four residents. Agency spokeswomen Cecilia Cavuto said the four expressed satisfaction about how the home was run. 'So our staff did not see any conditions which concerned them related to the health and safety of the residents,' she said.

One of the men found in the house on Whitecastle Lane had stayed four nights at a Coalition shelter in August 2010, although there was no other record of him.

'People fall into homelessness for many different reasons,' she said. 'It's often coupled with mental incapacities, physical disabilities.'

Then on 25 July came the news that one of the former captives, 79-year-old William Merle Greenawalt, had died just 11 days after his release. By then, 59-year-old Dean Cottingham and 64-year-old John Edward Padget had been released from LBJ General Hospital and were in the care of Adult Protective Services. The fourth man, 54 years old, told officers that he was a military veteran. He declined treatment but authorities said he would be cared for at a Veterans Administration hospital. He told reporters that he was living in the house and not the garage, although he said he had been sleeping on the floor.

Meanwhile, back in Ohio, a woman arrested for stealing a candy bar in Asland, just 50 miles from Cleveland, begged police to jail her alleging three people had been mean to her. She went on to tell the authorities that she and her five-year-old daughter had been locked in a basement for over two years in the two-storey weatherboard house.

Her four alleged captors were charged with kidnapping and extortion. One of the accused was also charged with three counts of weapons possession. The victim also alleged that they cashed her monthly disability cheque.

Ashland Police Chief David Marcelli said in the course of interviewing her, they gradually discovered the rest of the facts. She was jailed briefly for beating her daughter, but told the judge that her captors had forced her to do it. 'It's unlikely that, on her own, she would have done these horrible things to that child,' her attorney said.

An attorney for one of the defendants said that the woman concerned 'was never forced to do anything. She used this story to get out of trouble she was in.' It was also said that the victim and her alleged captors were friends and they had tried to help her by offering her a place to live because they were homeless. She was free to move in and out whenever she wanted.

County social services workers had placed the child with her mother while she lived in the suspect's house, and a neighbour said that he once gave the woman a lift when his daughter rented part of the house. 'She didn't say anything, didn't act any different,' he said. 'She has got a little different personality, but you would not have thought this was going on.'

12

THE BABY
FARM

A brutal precursor of Ariel Castro was Gary Heidnik, who held six women in the basement of his house in Philadelphia and repeatedly raped and tortured them. He went further, torturing two of them to death. The Amanda Berry figure who secured their release was a 25-year-old named Josefina Rivera. As a teenager, Josefina had dropped out of school and took to the streets. This made her tough enough to survive her ordeal and, eventually, outsmart her captor.

On the night of 25 November 1986, she had walked out on her boyfriend, Vincent Nelson, and was working the corner of Girard and Third in Philly's run-down north side. It was already 11.00pm, but she did not want to go home without turning at least one trick. The following day was Thanksgiving.

She had about given up when a brand-new, grey-and-white Cadillac Coupe De Ville pulled up. Behind the wheel was Gary Heidnik. The trick was a stranger, but expensively dressed. He offered $20 and she got in.

After a cup of coffee in McDonald's, he took her to his home at 3520 North Marshall Street in an area known as 'The OK Corral', at that time, after a shoot-out between drug dealers. In his garage there he had several other cars, including a Rolls-Royce. He also had an unusual door-locking system, which only he could work.

Inside the house, Heidnik asked if Josefina wanted to watch a pornographic video. She looked at her watch. A look of fury flashed across his face. She explained that she had three children at home and the babysitter was waiting. In reality, her children had been put up for adoption years earlier.

Upstairs, Heidnik flung the $20 at her and they had perfunctory sex. Josefina got up to get dressed when Heidnik suddenly grabbed her by the throat. He handcuffed her and dragged her downstairs into the cellar where he chained her, naked, to a pipe.

In the middle of the filthy cellar, there was a pit. Josefina feared that it would be her grave. She screamed. Heidnik slapped her and flung her down on a filthy mattress. Then he lay and slept like a baby with his head on her lap.

In the morning, Josefina managed to prise a plank off one of the boarded-up windows. She squeezed through it out into the garden and began to yell. But people were used to loud music and even the sound of gunshots coming from Heidnik's house. Nobody took any notice. It was that sort of area.

But Heidnik heard. He ran out and dragged her back into

the basement by her chains. He slung her in the pit, covered it with boards and sacking, and turned the radio up full blast. This was to be a regular punishment.

Heidnik was clearly disturbed. Born in 1943, his parents had split up when he was 17 months old after his father had accused his mother of being a drinker and a wild woman. Gary and his older brother Terry stayed with their mother during their school years, then they moved in with their father. He was a strict disciplinarian, who would even dangle Gary feet first from an upstairs window as punishment.

With an IQ of 130, Heidnik did well at school. He joined the boy scouts and said he was going to become a millionaire. Then, in his early teens, he fell out of a tree and suffered permanent brain damage. After trying to kill his brother and attempting suicide several times, Heidnik was committed to a mental hospital. From there, he went to a military academy, but flunked out after at least three more suicide attempts.

Life was so intolerable back with his father he cut all ties and enlisted in the Army, describing himself in his army papers as 'coloured' like his mother, who was a Creole. She had become an alcoholic and committed suicide in 1971. In the Army, Heidnik became a loan shark, but he was still exhibiting psychiatric symptoms. He was discharged with a 100 per cent disability pension of $2,000 a month. With this, he speculated on the stock market and, with his mathematical mind, he quickly made vast sums of money.

Apart from his collection of cars and expensive clothing, he spent vast amounts on pornographic magazines and books featuring black women, and he bought a house in an

African-American area giving him access to black prostitutes. One of the girls he picked up was Anjeanette Davidson who had an IQ of just 49. He got her pregnant, then refused to let her see a doctor and beat and starved her. When she was rescued by her sister, she was rushed to hospital. She gave birth by Caesarean section and the child was put into care.

Heidnik tried to shoot a man who rented a room in his house, but the charges were inexplicably dropped. When he moved, the new owners found stacks of pornographic magazines and a pit he had dug in the basement. The run-down neighbourhood he moved to was a good cover for his activities.

By 1978, Heidnik had been charged with kidnapping, rape, false imprisonment and involuntary deviant sexual intercourse. Anjeanette Davidson's sister Alberta was found locked in a garbage bin in Heidnik's basement. With an IQ of just 30, she was missing from the state mental hospital. But Alberta was deemed unfit to testify and Heidnik was sentenced to three to seven years for the lesser charges of abduction and assault.

Most of his sentence was spent in state mental institutions, but there was no one to keep an eye on him when he got out. And when Anjeanette Davidson disappeared, no one suspected Heidnik, although he was later thought to be responsible for her murder.

In 1985, he married a Filipina named Betty Disto, whom he had met through a matrimonial agency. Arriving from the Philippines, she found a black woman in Heidnik's bed. Then a week after their wedding, she found him having sex with three black women in their bedroom.

Other women were brought to the house and Betty was forced to watch him having sex with them. He starved her, beat her, refused her food, and forced her to have anal intercourse. After just three months, she went to the police. He was charged with indecent assault, rape and other felonies. But Betty was too afraid to turn up in court and the charges were dropped. She then sent a postcard, telling him that she was pregnant. He refused to pay maintenance, telling the family court he did not have a job.

Three days after Josefina arrived in Heidnik's basement, he forced her into the pit again and covered it over. Then he went out looking for 25-year-old Sandra Lindsay, a former lover he had known for four years. Like his other lovers, she was black, good-looking and classified as mentally retarded. He had a grudge against her – she had become pregnant by him years earlier. He had offered her $1,000 to keep the child, but she had had an abortion.

Heidnik found Sandra, brought her back to the house, stripped her naked and chained her up in the basement. Josefina was then hauled from the pit and Heidnik explained that the two of them were a baby farm. He planned to have ten black sex slaves in his basement. They were all going to give him babies who would grow up as 'one big happy family'. Then he raped Sandra and Josefina and forced them to perform other sexual acts with him. The rest of the night, he would spend digging out what he called the 'punishment pit'.

The next morning, Sandra's sister Teresa and two cousins knocked on Heidnik's door. He did not answer the door and they went away. Sandra's mother then went to the police, accusing Heidnik of holding her daughter. Heidnik took the precaution of forcing Sandra to write a postcard to her mother, telling her not to worry, she would call. He drove to New York where he posted it. Later, he sent a Christmas card, ostensibly from Sandra, enclosing a $5 bill.

Meanwhile the sex fell into a routine. First, the girl would have to stimulate him orally. Then, when he was ready to come, he would put his penis in one of the girl's vaginas and ejaculate there. As his aim was to impregnate them, he went to great lengths not to come in their mouths.

On 22 December 1986, he offered 19-year-old Lisa Thomas a lift to a friend's house where she had left her gloves. She was not a prostitute and he took her for a meal at TGI Friday's. Then he invited her to go with him to Atlantic City. She said she had nothing to wear, so he took her to Sears, where he bought her two outfits. He took her back to his house to try them on. He spiked her drink and she woke up naked on his waterbed. After they had sex, she wanted to leave, but he began choking her. Handcuffed, she was dragged naked down to the basement. There he pulled back the flooring and out clambered two naked black girls – Sandra and Josefina.

He got his captives some jam and peanut butter sandwiches. But before the starving girls could eat, he put them through a humiliating routine. They had to kiss his ass, lick his balls and suck his penis. Then he would have sex with them. Only afterwards were they allowed to eat.

There was other sexual activity going on upstairs. Once a week, a girl named Jewel came to his house. Usually, there would be another girl there. Heidnik would like to have sex with one of them, while biting on the other girl's breast. Jewel made only one proviso – he had to have sex with her first. She did not want his penis in her vagina after it had been inside the other girl.

On New Year's Day 1987, 23-year-old Deborah Dudley became his fourth sex slave. On the principle of divide and rule, he put one of the girls in charge while he was away. When he returned, they were to tell him who had committed any misdemeanours, then mete out the punishment he thought appropriate.

On 18 January, he brought home 18-year-old Jacquelyn Askins. Once more, after sex, he dragged her down to the basement and chained her up naked with the others. This time he beat her buttocks with a plastic rod to ensure future compliance.

With the girls chained and shackled, Heidnik raped them every day, penetrating them one after the other, until he climaxed or lost interest. As added stimulation, he would force them to have sex with each other.

On Josefina's birthday, she was allowed to pick a meal from the menu of a local Chinese restaurant. He also brought champagne for the girls, although he did not drink himself. They were to celebrate, he said, as he thought both Josefina and Sandra were pregnant. This proved not to be the case. Being half-starved, the girls could not conceive. This made Heidnik angry and he beat them.

As Sandra Lindsay had known him before, she proved the most troublesome. So he tied her wrists to an overhead beam and left her dangling there for a week. He kept her alive by force-feeding her, but eventually she choked on a piece of bread and died. When he cut her down, he kicked her dead body. Her corpse was left lying on the floor while he gave the other girls ice-cream.

Afterwards, he carried her over his shoulder upstairs. Soon, the smell of cooked flesh became overpowering. It was so strong that the neighbours complained to the police. A young officer knocked on the door. Opening it just a few inches, Heidnik explained that he had just burnt his dinner.

Deborah Dudley had also tried to resist Heidnik's sexual demands. He took her upstairs where he showed her Sandra's head boiling in a pot. Her ribs were in a roasting pan and other body parts were being prepared for the freezer. Heidnik told Deborah that if she did not submit, she would end up that way, too. He then fed the meat to his captives, while the bones were given to his dogs. Later, he added dog food to their meals of minced body parts.

The only other time the girls were allowed out of the basement, they were taken, one at a time, to be washed. Afterwards, they would have to perform a sexual act with Heidnik as a thank you before being returned to their shackles.

With the girls in the basement, Heidnik went about his normal life. He followed the stock market, kept in touch with his broker, visited car showrooms and went to court over his maintenance payments. He even went out on dates with his latest girlfriend, an African-American nurse.

While he was out, he took no chances. The girls were put in the punishment pit, which was covered with planks, weighed down with heavy sacks. Down there for long periods, they found it hard to breathe and would scream. As punishment, he would beat them. To mask their screams, he would play loud religious music day and night.

Worse punishments were to come. Still defiant, Deborah Dudley was pushed into the pit with Jacquelyn Askins and

Lisa Thomas. Josefina was told to pour water over them. Then Heidnik prodded their bodies with a live electric wire and Deborah was electrocuted.

Heidnik decided not to risk dismembering and cooking Deborah's body. Instead, he forced Josefina to sign a letter saying that she had killed Deborah and took her with him when he drove out into the wilds of New Jersey to dump the corpse.

By then, Josefina had seen Heidnik kill two other girls and realized that there was only one way to get out of the basement alive. He already seemed to favour her over the other girls, so she began to flirt with him, with the aim of becoming his confidante. But the other girls thought she was conniving with their jailer. This put their backs up.

Josefina won Heidnik's trust when she consented to join in his regular sexual encounters with Jewel. Heidnik began to take her out to McDonald's. He bought her wigs as a disguise and would never let her out of his sight. She was also warned that, if she tried to escape, he would kill the other three girls and, if the police ever caught up with him, he would plead insanity while she would get life for murdering Deborah because of the confession she had signed.

With two girls dead, Heidnik was on the lookout for new meat for his harem. He took a fancy to 24-year-old Agnes Adams whom Josefina knew from a strip club where they had both worked. Heidnik had tried to get her back to his house before. In January, he had offered her $35 for oral sex, but when they got back to his house, someone had parked across the driveway. In February, he had got her into the house, but let her go. So when, on 23 March, she saw

Heidnik in the car with Josefina, she had no reason to be wary. But back at the house, after Heidnik had had sex with Agnes, he choked her, handcuffed her and dragged her down to the basement.

Again, Josefina seemed to be colluding with their tormentor. The other girls had been planning to attack Heidnik with broken glass and lengths of pipe that littered the floor of the basement. When Heidnik discovered this, he beat them viciously and they assumed Josefina had betrayed them. Meanwhile, Heidnik had become paranoid about the women listening to him moving around the house and punctured their eardrums with a screwdriver. Only Josefina was spared, making the other girls resent her all the more.

She now put her escape plan into action. On 24 March 1987, after four months of captivity, she persuaded Heidnik to let her go and visit the three children she said she had when she had first come home with him. In return, Josefina promised to bring him a new woman for his baby farm.

As he dropped her off near her home, they agreed to meet at Girard and Sixth Street. If she was not there, it did not matter much. Who was going to believe the wild accusations of what he took to be a simple-minded whore? He was very nearly right.

Once Heidnik was out of sight, Josefina ran back to the apartment where she lived with her boyfriend, Vincent Nelson. He was still angry after the row they had had the night before Thanksgiving and was not prepared to listen to her babbling about naked girls being chained up in a basement. But then he noticed that she was terrified. If this guy Heidnik was responsible, he was going to sort him out. But on the way to Girard and Sixth, he realized that, if even a quarter of what Josefina said was true, Heidnik might be armed and dangerous. They stopped at a phone booth just one block from the rendezvous and called the police.

The desk sergeant was sceptical, but sent a patrol car. The officers in it did not believe her either, but took her to the police station. It was only when she showed them the scars and bruises on her body, and the marks from the shackles around her ankles, that they realized there might be something to her story. So a squad car was sent over to Girard and Sixth where a grey-and-white Cadillac was waiting. They arrested Heidnik at gunpoint. He did not resist, assuming that he was being arrested for non-payment of child maintenance.

Another squad car went to 3520 North Marshall Street. No one answered the door and, as they had no search warrant, there was nothing they could do. When a warrant came four hours later, the police crowbarred open the metal front door. In the front room, they found a huge collection of pornographic videotapes and erotic books showing naked black women. In the basement, they found two naked black women huddled under a blanket. They screamed, but could not run away as they were shackled and chained.

They pointed to large sacks in the middle of the floor. Under them they found another naked girl, handcuffed and squatting in a pit. All three were filthy and starving. In the fridge, an officer found a human rib.

The book was thrown at Heidnik. He was charged with indecent exposure, simple assault, aggravated assault, issuing terrorist threats, reckless endangerment, unlawful restraint, false imprisonment, criminal solicitation, indecent assault, rape, involuntary deviant sexual intercourse, two counts of murder, and the possession and abuse of a corpse. He also admitted several other murders.

In jail, he tried to commit suicide, and he was attacked by other prisoners. In court, his defence made what it could of the acrimony between the surviving victims. On the stand, Josefina appeared almost sympathetic to Heidnik's desire to have children, because the city had taken hers away.

Jacquelyn Askins was questioned about the extra-long chains on her shackles.

'He did that so I could open my legs for sex,' she said. She sobbed when she described the deviant group sex that the girls had been forced into and the beatings they had been subjected to.

The jury dismissed the defence's attempt to show that Heidnik was insane after his financial adviser from Merrill Lynch was called to testify. Heidnik was 'an astute investor who knew exactly what he was doing,' he said. The figures spoke for themselves.

They found Heidnik guilty of the first-degree murder of Sandra Lindsay and Deborah Dudley; he was also found guilty on six counts of kidnapping, five counts of rape, four counts of aggravated assault, and one count of involuntary deviant sexual intercourse. Indeed, he was found guilty on all the charges except for involuntary deviate sexual intercourse with Josefina Rivera. No explanation was given for his acquittal on that count.

The victims were awarded $34,000 each, while Betty Disto received $30,000 from her husband's estate. Heidnik was given two death sentences. His father said, 'I hope he gets the chair. I'll even pull the switch.'

THE DISAPPEARED

He was executed by lethal injection on 6 July 1999, the last person to be executed by the Commonwealth of Pennsylvania.

13

THE MILK CARTON KID

Tanya Nicole Kach became one of 'the disappeared' voluntarily – at first, at least. Her parents split up when she was 11. By 13, she had lost touch with her mother and her father had moved in with his girlfriend. They did not get along.

'My mother wasn't in my life at that point,' Tanya said. 'My dad completely forgot he even had a daughter and we were living under the same roof, and I was hanging around with the wrong crowd.'

She was attending Cornell Middle School in McKeesport, a suburb of Pittsburgh, Pennsylvania. One day, when she had to leave school early to pick up a project for her carpentry class, she was stopped by moustached security guard Tom Hose, who asked to see her hall pass. 'He was so nice, cracking jokes,' she said. 'After that, he became my confidant, talking to me about my home life.'

Although Tom was 37 – 24 years older than Tanya – she did not think that the age difference mattered. He was a good listener. 'He was an authority figure, wearing a uniform and a badge ... somebody that you would trust, and he befriended me.' Hose also gave her money and bought her sweets and cigarettes. After a few months, he kissed her under the school's stairwell and she fell in love. But Hose was also manipulating her.

She said that Hose told her, 'You're stupid. You're immature. Nobody cares about you but me.' She later came to realize that she was nothing but a puppet.

He persuaded her to run away from home and come to stay in the house, just two miles away, where he lived with his parents and his son who was only two years younger than her. However, they were not to know that she was there and she spent the next ten years hidden in his bedroom.

The conditions were primitive. 'He put a bucket in there, and said, "That's your bathroom,"' Tanya said. 'I was just so brainwashed. I feel humiliated now. Absolutely.'

Shut up in the room 24 hours a day, she was fed peanut butter and jelly sandwiches along with a banana and a can of Faygo soda pop. Sometimes, Hose smuggled up leftovers from his dinner. About twice a week in the dead of night, he took her down into a cellar with cold, concrete floors to take a shower. She also became his sex slave.

'When I first lost my virginity to him, I did what I was told,' she said. 'No matter what it was, I did what I was told.'

Hose recorded their sex sessions in a diary so that he could brag to his co-workers how often he had sex. A naïve young girl, she put up with the ordeal for the sake of love. 'I was fine at first,' she said. 'I thought I was in love and felt my sacrifices were a labour of my love for Tom Hose. Soon, however, the ordeal began to take its toll.'

Although he eventually allowed her a crumb of freedom, she did not dare to try and escape because, she said, he threatened to hunt her down and kill her. 'When my mind just completely went on me, I would sit there or I would imagine a childhood friend was there,' she said. 'I would put my ear to the vent to hear what his parents were talking about downstairs.'

The hardest times for the missing girl were holidays. She spent four Christmas Eves inside a closet upstairs in the Hose family home. 'It broke my heart,' she said. 'I thought of my family, wondering if they were thinking about me.'

After the first four years, he slackened the regime somewhat. She was then 18. He permitted her to go on the back porch while he was getting ready for work. But still his control over her was absolute. 'He would just point. I was like a dog,' she said. 'I did what my master told me. I went in the closet.'

Later, he forced her to dye her hair and change her name to Nikki Allen, then he told his parents that his new girlfriend Nikki was moving in. She was allowed to go to church and venture out during the day, but seeing outside life realized her living situation was not normal.

'I was scared,' she said. 'I came to realize other people's relationships weren't like that. I had to be home at 2.00pm every day.'

Hose also told people she was a year older than her actual age, although he did not change the date. 'He let me keep my birthday,' she said. 'I got to celebrate my birthday on my birthday.'

Hose's home was two blocks from JJ's Deli Mart in this Pittsburgh suburb, police said. For six months she would visit the store and talk to owner Joseph Sparico and his family. She was always neatly dressed, he said. 'She wanted to be wanted, that's all,' said Sparico. 'She'd come up to get a pop, a tea, a paper ... she'd confide in me.' Then, in March 2006, she told Sparico something extraordinary.

'My name is not Nikki Allen,' Tanya said in a frightened voice. 'It's Tanya Nicole Kach. If you go to a website for missing children, you will see me there.'

Sparico called his son, who was a retired police officer. He recognized Kach's name. Then he phoned a missing children hotline, eventually helping to reunite Tanya and her family. He said that Tanya had told him she was not allowed out after dark, and that she thought nobody wanted her other than Hose, who also threatened her.

Tanya's father, Jerry, said, 'I just say thank you ... there is a God and he brought my little girl back home.'

During the time she was missing, her picture was printed on the backs of milk cartons, alerting the public that she was a missing person. Later, she published a book about her imprisonment under the title *Memoir of a Milk Carton Kid*.

'The only way I survived was through God. I mean, God gave me the strength to get through it,' said Tanya. Describing the reunion with her father, she said, 'He's crying, I'm crying. All he kept saying was, "I got my baby." That night, I asked my dad to tuck me in, and I was a 24-year-old woman, and he did. That's all I wanted,' Tanya said.

Clutching her father's hand, she said, 'I'm touching blood, and I get to say, "I love you, Dad."'

The two were later estranged because of his 'negativity',

she said. He told her, 'If you want to go out and tell your story, go on trash TV and have your 15 minutes, fine. But don't drag me down with you and besmirch my good name.' She also said that he did not believe her account of being kept under total mental and physical control by Hose. Later, Jerry Kach told the *Pittsburgh Tribune Review*, 'I love my daughter. But her last words to me were, "Have a nice life, Jerry." Those words really hurt.'

Kach's wife said that Tanya had been a habitual runaway, while Tanya's mother, Sherri Koehnke, who remarried while her daughter was missing, said, 'It's the best ending I could have when I thought about what could have happened to her.'

James Warman, who lived on the same street as Hose, said that he had never seen Tanya until about eight months before she escaped. He said she was a sweet girl who would talk with people in the neighbourhood, but would hurry home in the early afternoon, before Hose got home from work. 'I don't want to say "nice guy", but that's what he seemed like,' he said. 'But now, you've got to look at him in a different light.'

Hose was charged with statutory sexual assault, three counts of involuntary deviate sexual intercourse, indecent assault, endangering the welfare of a child, corruption of a minor, interference with the custody of children and aggravated indecent assault. He was suspended without pay from the school where the two had met and where he had continued to work as a security guard.

His attorney insisted that Tanya was never held against her will. However, in court, Hose pleaded guilty to all charges. He apologized, telling the judge, 'Only God knows how sorry I truly am.' But he insisted that Tanya had repeatedly thanked him for taking care of her, saying, 'Without you, I'd be dead or in the streets.'

The judge replied, 'You give yourself clearly too much credit ... You see yourself as completely different than the rest of the world.'

And Tanya said that he had not done anything to help her, telling her often, 'Oh, you're just a pretty face. You're so stupid, you'd be nothing without me.'

In court, with tears welling in her eyes, she asked Hose in a faltering voice, 'I just want to know why you did what you did to me for ten years. Why?' She said that Hose had robbed her of her innocence. 'It's so sad to say, but I was a puppet, nothing but a puppet.' Hose had controlled what she ate, drank and wore. 'I am not that dominated puppet anymore,' she told him.

He was sentenced to five to 15 years. However, when the five years was up, he was refused parole.

After the hearing, Tanya said of the man she had once loved and trusted, 'He's an absolute monster. There's just no words to explain him.'

Tanya Kach completed her high-school education and went to college. However, she had missed out on that American right of passage – the high-school prom. She had cried about it while being held in captivity. 'I did think about it, many times, and I sat there and I cried knowing that I couldn't go,' Tanya said of those darkest days in her life. However, seven years after she escaped, her fiancé, Karl McCrum, heard about the 'Second Chance Prom' in Pittsburgh for those who had had a bad prom experience or had not had the opportunity to go. With the help of a local radio station, he secured tickets. Wearing a light-pink dress and a white corsage, the former captive's dream came true.

'I was so ecstatic to finally do something that I missed, and it felt like a hole inside of me was filled because it was something that was missing all those years,' she told ABC. 'It was so wonderful and magical and awesome. It meant the world to me, it really did … One of my dreams came true, and I got to go to the prom with the man that I love.'

14

BACKYARD SEX SLAVE

The most notorious case of sexual slavery in America was the kidnap and imprisonment of Jaycee Lee Dugard when, on 26 August 2009, it was discovered that she had been held, along with her two daughters, in the backyard of a house in California for over eighteen years.

Eleven-year-old Jaycee Lee Dugard had been abducted on 10 June 1991 on her way to catch the school bus from her home in South Lake Tahoe. Her stepfather Carl Probyn was watching as she walked up Washoan Boulevard. He noticed a grey sedan with a couple in it drive by. Suddenly, it did a U-turn. On the way, the driver rolled down his window as if to ask the girl for directions, then he leaned out of the door and grabbed her. Jaycee screamed and tried to get away. There was a cracking sound. Paralyzed by a stun gun, she was dragged into the back of the car ... a blanket was thrown over her ... someone sat on her and the car took off.

Seeing his stepdaughter being abducted in broad daylight, Probyn jumped on his bike and cycled after the car. But there was no way he could keep up or even get the licence number. Returning home, he called the police. He gave them a description of the car and the couple in it, but they were long gone.

Some way out of town, the car stopped. The woman who had been sitting on top of Jaycee moved into the front of the car. The man with her was laughing. He said he could not believe that they had got away with it. Jaycee was terrified.

When the car stopped again, Jaycee was bundled into a house under a blanket. She was told to keep quiet, otherwise she would be attacked by what sounded like some very aggressive dogs. In the bathroom, the man made her take her clothes off. He stripped off as well and made her touch him. In the shower, he shaved what little hair she had around her pudendum and in her armpits, while she cried. Wrapped a blanket, she was taken out into the back garden and found herself in a small room with egg crates for a bed. She was left there handcuffed to cry herself to sleep.

Within hours of Jaycee's abduction, the media descended on South Lake Tahoe. Dozens of volunteers searched the area. Tens of thousands of flyers and posters were handed out across the United States. At one stage, Carl Probyn was considered a suspect, but eventually he was ruled out. His marriage to Jaycee's mother Terry fell apart.

On the morning following the abduction, the man arrived with something to eat and drink, and a bucket Jaycee could use as a lavatory. Each time her abductor came to see her, he tried to win her over. She resisted. After about a week, he gave up. Soon after, he fastened the handcuffs behind her back, then he raped her.

Afterwards, she was bleeding. She was brought a washcloth and bucket of warm water to wash herself. It was the first of many times she would be raped and she soon learned to distance herself by thinking about something else until he had finished.

At first, she did not even know her tormentor's name. Gradually, she got to learn that it was Phillip and she even admitted to enjoying his company, when he was not using her for sex. At one point, she wondered whether he was her biological father whom she had never known.

Although air-conditioning had been installed, her backyard home was primitive. Unable to take a shower, she attracted ants and, with her hands cuffed, it was impossible to keep them away, or even brush her teeth. Eventually, Phillip left off the cuffs, but the door remained firmly locked. Some days he would play the guitar for her, saying he was going to be famous. Then he brought a small black-and-white TV and a cat for company, although it was taken away when it peed everywhere.

Phillip said that he had a 'problem' with sex that his wife, Nancy, could not help him with. He hurt other people and she was there so he would not hurt anyone else. Garrido later wanted Nancy to join in their sex sessions, and on one occasion he even wanted Jaycee to have sex with a dog.

One night, he took her into a larger room with a couch, a desk, a small fridge and a TV. There he took a cocktail of drugs and explained the terrible things that she was going to have to do to fulfil his depraved fantasies. She cried as she found herself plunged deeper into a nightmare of sexual abuse. That night she found herself bleeding again. She was having her first period.

Forty-year-old Phillip Garrido was also a registered sex offender. When he was just 18, the rumour circulated at school that he had raped a girl. His father said that, during his teens, he had had a motorcycle accident that changed him. Within a month of graduating, he was busted for the possession of cannabis and LSD. At 21, he plied a 14-year-old girl with drugs and took her to a motel and raped her, but the victim refused to testify and the charges were dropped.

After falling out with the local drug dealers, Garrido fled to South Lake Tahoe. His high-school sweetheart Christine Perreira went with him. They married and she supported them as a blackjack dealer in a casino.

For years, he took up to ten tabs of LSD a day. He beat Christine when she refused to go along with his plans to join in when he was having sex with multiple partners. But when another man flirted with her, he tried to stab her in the eye.

In 1976, he rented a storage locker and lined it with thick carpet to deaden any sound. On 26 November, he dropped four tabs of acid and tried to abduct a woman he had been stalking. When she escaped him, he drove to the casino where Christine worked and begged a lift off another blackjack dealer, 25-year-old Katherine Callaway. When they arrived at his 'home', she found they were actually at an empty lot. He smashed her head into the steering wheel and handcuffed her. Throwing a coat over her, he drove her to the lock-up. Inside was a mattress with a red satin sheet and an old kerosene can that she could use as a toilet. Then for five-and-a-half hours, he raped her repeatedly.

In the middle of the night, someone began banging on the door. Garrido said it was 'just the guy next door'. Not long after that, there was another bang on the door. 'I think it is the heat,' Garrido said. 'Are you to be good?'

Outside, Reno cop Clifford Conrad was questioning Garrido when Katherine ran out bruised, naked and crying, 'Help me.'

In court, Garrido blamed the LSD. He admitted masturbating in drive-in theatres, restaurants, bars, public restrooms, outside the windows of peoples' homes and, even more disturbingly, outside elementary schools in front of girls aged seven to ten. Garrido was sentenced to 50 years in the federal penitentiary at Leavenworth, Kansas. Christine divorced him. Inside, he became a Jehovah's Witness and it was thought that, because of his religious zeal, he would be unlikely to commit further crimes. He was paroled after just 11 years. Three years after his release, he kidnapped Jaycee Dugard.

To intimidate her, Garrido threatened to give her to other men, even worse than him, who would keep her in a cage. She had no choice but to do everything he wanted. He would tie her up, or videotape her doing degrading things.

After one day-long session of drug-fuelled sex, he let her remain in the larger room. There she was handcuffed to a pull-out bed. After a few months, she was unshackled. But the door was securely locked and there were iron bars on the windows. Again, there was no running water and she still had to use a bucket as a lavatory.

Eventually, Jaycee was introduced to Nancy. Garrido wanted them to be good friends. She had been visiting her uncle in jail when she met Garrido and they were married by the prison chaplain. When he was paroled in 1988, they moved in with Garrido's mother who lived just outside Antioch, California. Her modest home had a secluded backyard where Jaycee was held.

While Jaycee was 'celebrating' her 12th birthday, her mother Terry founded a group called Jaycee's Hope to keep her case in the public eye. Her kidnap appeared several times on *America's Most Wanted*, but no one had a clue where she was and few believed she was still alive.

After the first year, Phillip, Nancy and Jaycee spent more time together, eating fast food and watching movies. Nancy was kind, but Jaycee did not think she really liked her. Then in April 1993, the police found drugs in the house and Garrido was sent back to jail for violating his parole conditions. But Nancy clung on to Jaycee. Garrido returned after four weeks with an electronic tag on his ankle.

The sexual abuse started again, but Garrido spent more time reading the Bible. Sometimes Jaycee was sent back into the smaller room when Garrido's friends came over to smoke weed and play music all night. She was also hidden there when Garrido said there were police in the area. One night, she was even smuggled out and hidden in a trailer where, for once, she found she had a proper bathroom with running water and a flush toilet.

In the spring of 1994, Jaycee began to put on weight and Phillip and Nancy said they thought she was pregnant. She was just 14 and hoped that she would be sent to a hospital, but Nancy was a nurse's aide, so she and Garrido delivered Jaycee's baby girl. They often took the baby away as if it were their own, leaving Jaycee to plumb new depths of loneliness.

Garrido's drug intake lessened but the sex sessions continued. Garrido insisted that one day she would enjoy them. Her only consolation was that she was saving other little girls going through the same ordeal. Nancy told her that they drove secretly videotaping little girls, whom Nancy would sometimes lure into the back of the van.

Jaycee's first daughter was three and still being breastfed when the teenager fell pregnant again. The second child was also a girl. She had a growth above her eye that should have been examined by a doctor.

Garrido erected a tall fence around the yard, so Jaycee and the children could go outside. Eventually, Jaycee was allowed outside in the backyard unsupervised. But escape was still not a possibility; she could hardly leave the children behind. Besides, Garrido had implanted the idea that the world was full of rapists and paedophiles even worse than him.

To support his growing family, Garrido set up a printing business and employed Jaycee, again as a slave. She also did design work, which filled up her spare time when she was not educating the children. Garrido also insisted that Jaycee's daughters called Nancy 'Mommy', while Jaycee was 'big sister'. In case clients twigged who she was, Jaycee was called 'Allissa'. Her hair was cut and dyed brown, and she was allowed out to the beach and on other family outings. At home, Garrido erected tents in the backyard to give Jaycee and the girls more living space. He allowed her to take a kitten to the vet, provided she pretended to be his daughter.

When Garrido's mother became ill, he let the two girls stay in the house to keep her company. Later, Jaycee was allowed into the house to help Nancy look after his mother. Although it was better than living in the backyard, the house itself was falling apart. The drains backed up and it was impossible to keep clean.

A new parole agent was assigned to Garrido and saw one of the girls asleep in the house. Jaycee herself even got to talk to another visiting parole agent. But although he was a registered sex offender nothing was said.

Garrido started talking about setting up a church called 'God's Desire' which would provide a remedy for rapists and paedophiles. He felt passionately that the nation needed to hear his teachings. On 24 August 2009, he went to the FBI office in San Francisco and delivered a rambling four-page essay called *Schizophrenia Revealed* which showed how sexual predators like him could be cured. He had been told this by mysterious voices he had picked up with the help of a device he had made. This turned out to be nothing but a cassette recorder inside a black box. Garrido, a registered sex offender, had taken the girls with him on the visit.

They were with him when he visited the University of California in Berkeley to ask for permission to stage an event for God's Desire on the campus. Events manager Lisa Campbell was suspicious and got campus police officer Ally Jacobs to do a background check on Garrido. When he discovered that Garrido had a rape conviction, she contacted his parole office.

Two parole officers were sent to Garrido's house. They searched it, but found only Nancy and his mother; they did not look out in the backyard. Then they took Garrido to the parole office where he explained that the two girls had been the daughters of a relative. Garrido had been barred from being in the company of minors and was required to return to the parole office the following day.

In his hubris, Garrido took Nancy, Jaycee and the girls with him. When she was questioned, Jaycee gave her name as Allissa. She said that she was the girls' mother and she had given him permission to take them with him the previous day, even though she knew he was a sex offender. But the parole officers accused her of lying to him. Garrido had said that 'Allissa' was their older sister.

Garrido had told her that, if anything went wrong, she should ask for a lawyer. The parole officer asked why she needed a lawyer if she had done nothing wrong. Garrido then confessed to kidnapping her. Jaycee was asked for her name again. In a shaky hand, she wrote down 'JAYCEELEEDUGARD'.

The spell was broken. The police phoned her mother and they had a tearful reunion the following day.

Garrido now became a 'person of interest' in the cases of other missing girls and the backyard of 1554 Walnut Avenue was searched. Behind a tarpaulin, they found a secret compound surrounded by tall trees and a 6ft-high fence. In it, there was a barn and sheds, one of which was sound-proofed and had been used as a makeshift prison.

Although Garrido had confessed to the police, in jail he was unrepentant. 'In the end, this is going to be a powerful, heart-warming story,' he told Walt Gray of KCRA-TV in a telephone interview and directed him to the documents he had lodged with the FBI, 'because what you are going to have in your hands will make world news immediately ... Wait 'til you hear the story of what took place at this house,' he went on. 'And you're going to be absolutely impressed.

It's a disgusting thing that took place with me in the beginning. But I turned my life completely around.'

Initially, Garrido and Nancy pleaded not guilty to charges including kidnapping, rape and false imprisonment, although they had both made full confessions. Then when the case came to trial on 28 April 2011, they both pleaded guilty to kidnapping and sexual assault, so Jaycee and her daughters were spared the ordeal of testifying. Not that Jaycee would have shrunk from that.

Phillip Garrido was sentenced to 431 years; Nancy 36 years to life. Jaycee and her family had already been awarded a $20 million settlement in 2009 through the state's victim's compensation fund. As therapy, Jaycee wrote the book entitled *A Stolen Life*.

15

THE SERIAL
SLAVE MASTER

In upstate New York, John Jamelske succeeded in kidnapping five women and holding them as his personal sex slaves in a career as an abductor that lasted over 15 years. But unlike Ariel Castro or Gary Heidnik, he took his captives one by one, releasing his victims when he grew tired of them. Some were so intimidated they did not report their ordeal; others had no idea where they had been held and could not lead the police there. It was only when Jamelske's self-belief led him to think it was safe to go out and about with his fifth victim that he was caught red-handed and the whole sordid story was revealed.

Born an only child in the village of DeWitt, now a suburb of Syracuse, in 1935, John Jamelske went to school in nearby Fayetteville. Withdrawn and bullied, he avoided sports and performed poorly in most subjects. His father was a horologist, and the young John later graduated with a degree in watchmaking.

THE SERIAL SLAVE MASTER

In 1959, he married schoolteacher Dorothy Richmond, who gave him three sons. Jamelske supported his family with a series of blue-collar jobs, supplementing his income by foraging for discarded bottles and cans, returning them by the thousand for the deposit, and cutting the coupons from newspapers in the local library.

However, he was actually a wealthy man. He had persuaded his father to invest in the booming stock market of the late fifties and early sixties. When his parents died, he inherited the lot. Then a series of real-estate deals made him a multi-millionaire. Even so, he was well known locally as the dishevelled old man dressed in a hooded sweatshirt and jeans who collected bottles and junk.

He had sold off the land surrounding his home to a developer who built an upmarket estate. Meanwhile, Jamelske let his blue-shingled, ranch-style home run to wrack and ruin, although he built a 6ft fence around the acre he had retained.

By the late 1980s, Jamelske's sons had grown up and left home, and his wife became bedridden. Jamelske seemed to go through some sort of midlife crisis. He began to wear designer jeans and tied his hair back in a ponytail. When he started to bring home a teenage blonde named Gina, his wife suspected that he was having an affair.

On 17 September 1988, Jamelske was cruising the streets of downtown Syracuse in his beat-up 1975 Mercury Comet when he saw a 14-year-old Native American girl named Kirsten walking along South Geddes Street. He stopped and offered her a lift. Friends advised her not to go with him, but she wanted a ride to a friend's house and he looked harmless enough. However, he took her home, stripped her naked and chained her up. When she protested, he threw her down a well and kept her there.

Her family reported her missing, but she had run away from home before. The police interviewed those who knew her, but there was no clue as to where she might have gone; she had simply disappeared.

Keeping a girl in a well was not very convenient, especially when he wanted to have sex with her, so he began building an underground bunker to keep her in. He brought in heavy machinery to dig a large hole in the backyard, lined it with concrete, then covered it over. Access was from his garage via a series of steel doors. Though the Cold War was thawing, neighbours assumed he was building a nuclear air-raid shelter.

Kirsten was imprisoned in two basement rooms with no windows. There was no plumbing and she had a bucket as a lavatory. Although there was no escape, she remained in chains and was further intimidated when Jamelske showed her pictures of her house and told her that he was going to kill her younger brother.

She was raped and sexually assaulted every day. As further humiliation, he recorded details of this abuse. Between assaults there were endless hours of boredom, spent waiting for her tormentor to come and rape her again.

Jamelske developed the delusion that they had a boyfriend–girlfriend relationship and brought her gifts, although he only fed her crackers and water. Later, her diet was supplemented with Kool-Aid.

Meanwhile, he cleverly allayed the concern of her family by forcing her to write a series of notes which he posted from New York and elsewhere. An audio tape of her saying,

'I can't wait to see you,' was sent and a message was left on a friend's answering machine, saying that she was going to return home soon.

In 1990, Jamelske decided to release her. But first he took her on holiday to Lake Tahoe. After a week, he gave her a ticket back to Syracuse and sent her home. But Kirsten was still frightened that Jamelske might hurt her little brother and nothing of what had happened to her was reported to the police.

Jamelske went on with his life as if nothing had happened. But nearly five years later, on 31 March 1995, he was cruising downtown Syracuse again when he saw a 14-year-old Latina on Catherine Street. He stopped and asked her to deliver a package for him. Naïvely, she got into his car. Back at DeWitt, he told her that the package was in the basement under the garage. When she went to get it, she found the door slammed behind her. After leaving her for hours in the dark to intimidate her, he persuaded her to take some pills. When she came to, she found herself chained to the wall, naked, and he took photographs of her lying naked and helpless on the floor.

He showed her pictures of her home and family – he knew where they lived and he would kill them if she did not do what he said. He had sold other girls into sexual slavery abroad, he said. She had no choice but to submit to him every day, while he fortified himself with Viagra. Once a week, he hosed her down with cold water.

Her family reported her missing. As far as the police were concerned, she was just another runaway and her details disappeared into their files.

After two years, Jamelske decided to release her. He drove

her blindfolded to her mother's apartment block and dropped her there for a tearful reunion. She told her mother that she had been held in a dungeon and raped every day and even gave a description of the man who had abducted her to the police but they soon dropped the investigation. For weeks afterwards, Jamelske drove by their home, but they were so intimidated, they did not report this to the police.

His next victim would be older. On 30 August 1997, he was cruising Syracuse when he saw a 52-year-old Vietnamese woman on Lodi Street. A refugee, she spoke little English. He appeared friendly and she got into his car. He took her to an abandoned house where he raped her, then he trussed her up in a cardboard box and took her back to his dungeon.

While her boyfriend reported her missing, she was an adult, not an underage girl, and the police were not obliged to undertake anything more than a perfunctory investigation.

Again, she was raped every day and made to do menial tasks such as stringing bottle caps on a wire, sewing quilts and sorting piles of screws and loose change. However, Jamelske bought her a TV so she could watch shows in the evening.

He claimed later that she sang to him in Vietnamese. She admitted that she was pleasant to him because she was intimidated. He made her sleep next to a life-size skeleton beside her on the mat she was forced to use as a bed. And there was physical violence; he hit her so hard that it left her partially deaf.

After nine months' captivity, he blindfolded her and

dropped her off at the Greyhound. She went straight to the police, but she had no idea where she had been and her description of her abductor barely fitted Jamelske. Later, Jamelske claimed that he had been doing her a favour, giving her a roof over her head.

On 11 May 2001, he saw Jennifer, a 26-year-old mother of two small children. Jamelske offered her a lift. She came to find herself naked in the dark in a cold room. When she resisted his attempts to rape her, he burnt her back with a cigarette. To intimidate her, he claimed he was part of a syndicate and he threatened to sell her if she did not do everything he wanted. Others would treat her far worse than he did. The police were involved; he showed her a fake sheriff's badge. When she was reported missing, the police sent out a helicopter to search the area where she was last seen. They came up with nothing. Again, Jennifer had simply disappeared.

Like the others, Jennifer was forced to sleep on a piece of foam matting and go to the toilet in a bucket. He fed her once a day, like a dog, and gave her a bath every two weeks, but the bathtub was not plumbed in. It drained on to the floor making living conditions damp and intolerable.

Rape was a daily affair. If she resisted, she was told it would add time to how long he would hold her. After sex, he would read the Bible to her for hours on end. She thought of knocking him out, but there was a combination lock on the door so this would be of no use. There was always suicide, but she did not want to die alone in a cellar without her children even knowing of her passing.

He afforded her certain kindnesses – installing cable TV and allowing her to write home to let her children know she was still alive. She had to say that she was in a rehab clinic.

The cigarette burns on her back became infected and, after just two months, he decided to let her go. But when he came down to the dungeon with her clothes, she was convinced he was going to kill her. Instead, he bundled her into the car, handcuffed and hooded, and dropped her off outside her mother's home.

Like previous captives, Jennifer could not tell the police where she had been held. However, she could describe the dungeon, saying there was a huge peace sign painted on the wall with the words 'WALL OF THUGS' in red alongside it. She also said that her abductor's car was a 1974 Mercury Comet. But the only 1974 Mercury Comet registered in New York State did not belong to Jamelske; his car was the 1975 model. The police closed the case, but some of the details lodged with Detective Jack Schmidt of the Onondaga County Sheriff's Department Abused Persons Unit.

After enslaving a Native American, a Latina, an Oriental and a Caucasian, Jamelske wanted an African-American. In October 2002, he saw a 16-year-old black girl on the corner of Elk Street and Salina Street. After a brief conversation, she got into his car. Later, he claimed that she was a prostitute. She denied it. Back at DeWitt, he threw her in his dungeon, stripped her naked, shredded her clothes and raped her.

He told her that there were vicious dogs outside that would kill her if she tried to escape. But he also said that he would release her, first on 17 November, then on Christmas Day. But those days came and went, and the sexual abuse continued. And what was just as appalling, her family had not even reported her missing and no one was looking for her.

Again, Jamelske seemed to develop an affection for his captive, whom he decided to call Meikka. Unlike the other victims, she was allowed upstairs into the house and even slept his bedroom. However, the windows were barred with the shelves out of an old fridge nailed to the frames. She was even allowed to go to the lavatory on her own as there were planks nailed across the windows in the bathroom.

But the daily rapes continued. The sex was often videoed and she was forced to fulfil his every desire.

But like Josefina Rivera before her, Meikka was cleverer than her captor and gave the impression that he could trust her. They would go shopping in nearby towns, go out to play pool or go bowling, take a walk around the neighbourhood and go to church together. On 3 April 2003, they went to the karaoke night at Freddy's Bar and Grill in Mattydale. Meikka sang three numbers to a crowd of over one hundred. However, she was young and intimidated, and Jamelske stood close beside her while she was on stage.

On the morning of 8 April, he took her with him to the bottle redemption centre in Manlius. While he was doing business, she persuaded him to let her use the phone. She said she wanted to call the church to check on the times of the services. Instead, she called her older sister and told her what had happened to her. When her sister called the number back, she asked the employee who answered the phone to call 911. The police arrived and asked Jamelske what he was doing with a young black girl. He said they were friends.

At the station, Jamelske admitted to having had sex with Meikka, saying it was consensual. However, she was 16 and the legal age of consent in New York State was 17. Meikka, of course, told a different story and Jamelske was charged with kidnapping, rape and sodomy.

The police went to search his home and found that Jamelske had erected a 10ft pole outside with the replica of a human head on it. From the ends of a crossbeam dangled chains. Behind another shelf unit full of bottles in the garage, Detective Schmidt and his partner Detective Eddie Bragg found a steel door. At the end of a short crawl-way was another steel door. When they opened it, they found a foul-smelling dungeon. It was damp and cold and, on the end wall, Schmidt saw on the wall a huge peace sign and the words 'WALL OF THUGS' in red. He realized its significance immediately.

The house itself was stacked with garbage. Among it, the police found videotapes of Jamelske with his victims. They also found calendars. Beside the dates, victims had been forced to write the letter 'S' when they had sex, 'B' when they bathed and 'T' when they were allowed to brush their teeth. They covered a period of 15 years.

Jamelske insisted that he had never hurt anyone, while his lawyers spent days explaining to him that abducting women from the streets and holding them in a dungeon was wrong. Eventually, Jamelske pleaded guilty to five counts of first-degree kidnapping, saving his victims from having to testify. However, at the sentencing hearing, the district attorney read the victims' statements into the court record.

'I am haunted every moment, even in sleep, by the thought of my months with Mr Jamelske,' wrote Kirsten. 'The cold, dampness, darkness and loneliness. I will never forget the constant hunger, thirst and fatigue. The thought of death ... I cannot speak of the terrible things he did to my body and made me do to his ... When I think of the things I have had to do just to stay alive, I cannot believe I am still here.' The DA added, 'The threats and intimidation ... left her with great fears and anxiety that have impacted and directed her life for the many years that followed.'

Jennifer said, 'I have lived my life for two years knowing that sick old man has existed and has done to other girls what he has done to me. I have lived in fear ever since ... John Jamelske is a sick and evil old man and should be punished. He has no right to take away my freedom, my right to breathe fresh air or my right to be treated like a human being. He made my children think I was dead. That hurts more than everything else in the whole world. They had to endure pain, so let his punishment be swift and just. Maybe then, I will at least be able to sleep at night.'

Meikka's statement said, 'I almost gave up hope when you brought my clothes to me in a million shredded pieces, telling me that these people trained those dogs to go after my scent. I felt completely stripped down to nothing ... You will never be able to know the fear I felt, being raped every day, sometimes three times a day. The nightmares I have, remembering how I had to fulfil your sick fantasies, making disgusting videos, being humiliated, never having any privacy, not even to use the toilet or the shower ... being chained to a fence like a dog. I hope with time I will be able to forget the horrifying sex you forced me to have day after day after day, relentless, for six-and-a-half long months, never leaving me alone, not for one day. You are the sickest man I have ever known ... I hope you die in a cold cement cell like you wanted us to do.'

Jamelske's Vietnamese victim said, 'I am haunted every

moment, even in sleep, by the thought of my months with Mr Jamelske. I now pray to my God that I am alive, that no one else will have to see the rooms in which I lived, and a part of me died.'

Throughout this, Jamelske appeared indifferent, enraging the judge. 'You are a sick coward,' he said. 'You're an evil man. You're a kidnapper and a rapist and a master manipulator of people and the truth. You took your American dream and turned it into a nightmare for these five women. Your reign of terror is over!' Jamelske was then sentenced to 18 years to life. 'There is no question in my mind you should die in prison for what you have done to these five women,' the judge said.

Jamelske was sent to Clinton Prison at Dannemora, the end of the road for New York's worst criminals. His assets were sold off and the money given to his victims. Interviewed in jail, Jamelske was unrepentant. He told the Syracuse *Post-Standard* that his victims were prostitutes, claiming later that they became his 'buddies'.

16

SLAVE IN
A BOX

Perhaps one of the most extreme cases of sexual slavery was that of Colleen Stan who was kept in a box under a bed for seven years and let out occasionally to be tortured and raped by a sexual sadist.

Colleen's captivity began on 19 May 1977. The 20-year-old Colleen Stan was hitch-hiking from Eugene, Oregon, to go to a friend's birthday party in Westwood, California, some 300 miles away. By mid-afternoon, she had reached Red Bluff, California, some 70 miles from her destination. Several young women had been murdered in the area, but Colleen considered herself an experience hitch-hiker. She was suspicious of lone male drivers, and turned down two potential rides. But then a 1971 two-door, cobalt-blue Dodge Colt with a man and a woman nursing a baby stopped. They said they were going to Westwood, and Colleen felt safe enough to get in.

The married couple were Cameron and Janice Hooker, although they did not volunteer their names. Cameron asked why she was going to Westwood. When she said that it was for a friend's birthday, he asked whether she was expected.

'No,' said Colleen. 'It will be a complete surprise.'

Already, she was beginning to feel that there was something weird about him. Indeed, from an early age, Cameron had been hooked on violent pornography. A year after he had graduated from high school, he met 15-year-old Janice. Cameron persuaded her to join in bondage games and S&M. She let him tie her naked to a tree, and even suspended her painfully by the wrists. They married and moved into 1140 Oak Street in Red Bluff. Their landlords, an elderly couple, lived next door. For them, the ostensibly respectable Hookers seemed the perfect tenants.

Janice grew tired of their bondage games and wanted to have a baby. She could have one, Cameron said, if she would help him find a young female slave to take her place. There would be no sex with the victim, Cameron promised; that would be saved for his wife. The slave was only there to be chained, beaten and tortured.

When they saw Colleen hitch-hiking outside Red Bluff, she seemed the perfect candidate. He hoped she would be the first of many.

Beside Colleen on the seat was a strange wooden box with leather hinges. Soon she would learn what this was for. The Hookers suggested they took a little detour to see some spectacular ice caves. They pulled off down a dirt road.

Stopping by a creek, Janice got out with the baby to get some cool water. Cameron followed; Colleen remained in the car. Suddenly, Cameron jumped in beside her and put a large butcher's knife to her throat. He handcuffed her hands behind her back and blindfolded her. A harness was put over her head with a broad leather strap across her mouth. Another strap passed under her chin, so she could not open her mouth to scream.

He tied her ankles together, so there was no chance that she could escape. The strange box was put over her head. It was filled with foam rubber, making breathing difficult and she became disorientated. Cameron then lay her down on the back seat, covering her with her own sleeping bag. Soon she began to overheat.

Once Janice and the baby were back in the car, they drove back to the highway and on towards Red Bluff. On the way, the couple stopped for a picnic. Colleen could smell food cooking. At the next stop, Colleen's ankles were untied and she was led into a house. In the basement, she was force to stand on an ice chest. Cameron then handcuffed her right wrist to a pipe above her head and started removing her clothes, finishing the task by strapping her left wrist to a wooden beam.

When she was naked with both arms strapped above her in the shape of a Y, he ran his hands over her body. She was sure she was going to be raped. Instead, he suddenly kicked the ice chest away, leaving Colleen suspended by her arms. It was agony. From under the blindfold, she saw a magazine on a table below her. It showed a naked women suspended from the ceiling, just as she was. Then she saw Cameron and Janice having sex on the table in front of her.

When Cameron noticed she was looking at them, he beat her mercilessly with a whip. This excited him and more sex ensued. Afterwards, Janice put her clothes on and went back upstairs while Cameron ran his hands over Colleen's naked body again. Then he took photographs of her and chained her up in a box. When she complained that she could hardly breathe, he threatened to sever her vocal cords. He had done it before, he said. She then felt something probing between her legs. Later, she discovered that he was trying to administer an electric shock to her genitals, but he could not get the equipment to work.

During the night, she was left trussed up, unable to move. Occasionally, he would come to admire the red welts left by the whip or run his hands over her body.

In the morning, she was released from the box and Cameron said he would let her go soon. For an hour, he left her chained up spread-eagled on a table with her head in a box. Then he released her and handed her a plastic bedpan. She had not relieved herself for 24 hours.

After he had fed her, he left her suspended from a beam for another 15 minutes. Then she was chained to a rack with her head back in the box, so she never knew if she was alone or if he was ogling her naked body.

When she complained of the cold the next day, a blanket was put over her. But when she refused a sandwich, he said she should be more grateful, suspended her from the ceiling and whipped her until she passed out. Absolute obedience was obligatory and she was returned to the rack where he taught her there was to be no whimpering and no conversation.

From then on she would spend 23 hours chained to the rack with the head box keeping her in complete isolation. Then she would be released to use the bedpan – with

Cameron watching. Two or three times a week she would be suspended from the ceiling or subjected to some other sadistic form of punishment and photographed in the most humiliating and degrading positions.

Any form of resistance or complaint would be punished. Once, when she was on the rack, she rattled the chains because she needed the bedpan. Afterwards, she was suspended from the ceiling and thrashed with a bullwhip for making a noise.

After a week, Cameron began constructing a coffin-shaped box, which would be Colleen's new home. It had a double skin to make it escape-proof. It was made from chipboard, which chafed her skin and gave her splinters. Air was provided by a hairdryer with the heating element turned off. Grease was put in her ears so she could hear nothing and she was kept in chains even in the box to make her feel even more helpless.

Confined there for 23 hours at a time, sometimes she would soil herself. The punishment was to be strung up and whipped with anything from a bullwhip to a cat-o'-nine tails. And there were other tortures. With her suspended from the ceiling, Cameron would burn her or administer electric shocks to vulnerable parts of her naked body. Sometimes, she would be strung up by the ankles. He drew his inspiration from S&M magazines and used her as a human guinea pig.

The Hookers would sometimes have sex on top of the box with Colleen inside it. Seemingly outside their agreement, Cameron would force Colleen to perform oral sex on him. As a reward, after three months, he brought her a tooth-brush and let her clean her teeth.

Due to stress, her periods ceased. When they resumed, she received a whipping, but she was also taken upstairs for a bath. Throughout the procedure, she was gagged with duct tape and blindfolded with a baby's nappy. Her hair was so filthy and tangled that Janice took a pair of scissors and cut it off.

But the relief at being clean after months of captivity was soon marred. Cameron hog-tied Colleen with her hands and feet behind her back. Then she was suspended from a boom handle and dunked head first in the water. She would be left there until she thought her lungs were exploding, pulled out for a second before being dunked back. This water torture lasted for two hours. Back on the rack, she was forced to fellate Cameron, and was then returned to the mind-numbing darkness and isolation of the box. After that, she was allowed a bath once a month and had to go through the water torture one more time. Throughout, she remained blindfolded, so she never knew whether she was being watched and there was no possibility of escape.

For first few months, Colleen did not even know the name of her captors. But then the man let slip the name 'Jan' when he asked his wife to pass him a small whip. Jan would sometimes whip her, too, and prod her with a sharp object, but she did not seem to get the same pleasure out of sadism as her spouse.

One night, Colleen was let out of her box and she was set to work sanding a knotty burl, albeit with a heavy box strapped on her head. She assumed these burls were being varnished and sold to bring money into the household.

Later, she was locked in a small workshop under the stairs and set to work shelling walnuts. She was allowed to take her blindfold off and, for the first time in six months, she could see. At first, Cameron put handcuffs around her ankles, but they swelled up so badly they had to be dispensed with. After that, she would be kept in the box during the day. In the evening, she would be fed some leftovers. Then her captor would inflict some pain on her for his own amusement. She spend the nights in the workshop doing some manual task with her blindfold off and a bedpan that she could use whenever she liked. But sometimes, it appeared that there was no work to be done and she was left in the box all day.

That year, Christmas was followed by Colleen's 21st birthday; then came the New Year. She spent all three occasions in her box in the cold of the basement.

One night, she was in the workshop when her torturer came to visit her. For the first time since he had held a knife to her throat, he let her see his face. She also noticed that he was wearing a belt with the name 'CAMERON' engraved on it.

He told her that a man from 'The Company' was upstairs and showed her a newspaper article about women being sold as slaves in the United States. Any who resisted were sent to Rent-A-Dungeon in San Francisco for 'remedial training'.

Cameron then produced a document dated 25 January 1978. It purported to be a contract between 'Colleen Stan, hereafter known as Slave, and Michael Powers, hereafter known as Master'. It required her to give herself to her slave master, body and soul. She must do everything she was told without question and every part of her belonged to him. She was not to wear underwear, or anything at all without his permission. Nor was she to cross her legs in his presence. Colleen was forced to sign it and the contract was witnessed by Janice, who signed as 'Janet Powers'.

Colleen noticed Janice's knees were bandaged and asked what was wrong with his wife's knees. Cameron explained that she had been a slave and had tried to escape. Taken to Rent-A-Dungeon she was nailed up ready to be tortured to death. He saw her there, took pity on her, bought her and married her, but her knees had been badly damaged during the punishment.

He added that when another slave had run away, The Company tracked down her family and tortured her mother until she revealed the whereabouts of her daughter. The runaway's fingers and toes were pulled off, and her arms and legs were amputated without anaesthetic. Her eardrums were punctured and her eyeballs burned out with a soldering iron. Her torso was then suspended by her braided hair from a hook on the ceiling of her master's bedroom. It took her a year to die. After what Colleen had been through already, this sounded all too credible.

After she signed the contract, she was given the slave name 'K'. This was emblazoned on her slave collar. A laminated card came from The Company, showing that she had been registered. Cameron told her that he had paid $1,500 to register her. The Master was now to be addressed as 'Sir', while Janice, the Mistress, must be called 'Ma'am'. She had to ask permission even to go the lavatory and, to address them, she had to kneel and look at the floor.

Colleen was then allowed upstairs to wash dishes and clean up. While doing her chores, she came across some correspondence from The Company complaining of her poor performance. All this helped convince her that The Company did exist.

The Master wanted to keep her naked, but the Mistress said she must wear a nightgown upstairs in front of their daughter. But at any moment Cameron might shout, 'Attention!' whereupon she was to strip off her nightgown and brace herself in the doorway, so he could whip her for minor infractions.

In February 1978, Colleen was tied spread-eagled on the Hookers' waterbed and left blindfolded. She felt Cameron and Janice kissing her all over her body. Then Cameron tried to rape her. But Janice fled into the bathroom and her husband went to comfort her. After that, Janice made great efforts to humiliate Colleen, as if she was a threat to her marriage.

On 28 April 1978, Colleen was left in the workshop all day. That night, she was taken out of the house, blindfolded, and driven to a mobile home nearby. There, she was put in another box, smaller than before, which fitted under the couple's bed. She was allowed a bedpan in there, but the stench would be overwhelming. Between the inner and outer skins, she found a picture of another girl and wondered if she had been an earlier victim. If there were no chores or Cameron's appetite for inflicting pain was sated, Colleen would be left in the box for 23 hours a day.

In the late spring, she was given denim shorts, a tank-top and a pair of tennis shoes so she could go out of the trailer to dig a trench to run the utilities to the trailer. Cameron's brother Dexter visited. Cameron told her he and their father Harold were also involved in The Company. They had a large dungeon in Arkansas where they tortured 26 slaves.

THE DISAPPEARED

Colleen was told not to act like a slave in front of family members. There was to be no kneeling and she was not to walk around nude. If they knew she was a slave, they would borrow her, Cameron said, and it would be the worse for her. She was to say that she was their housekeeper and babysitter.

One day, Harold arrived unexpectedly to find Colleen scrubbing the trailer floor. Janice rushed her into the bedroom and got her to put some clothes on. Cameron then pretended to take 'Kay' home. Instead, he locked her in a storage shed. In due course, Colleen was introduced as Kay to Janice's parents, too, and they did not notice anything amiss.

That summer, Colleen enjoyed working in the garden. The Hookers always kept a close watch on her. Meanwhile, Cameron had constructed a reinforced frame to which she could been strapped for bondage sessions. The problem was that his family might drop round any moment and their daughter was getting bigger, so Cameron constructed a second storage shed in the garden. There, Colleen could be stripped, blindfolded, gagged, strung up and whipped. During one of the torture sessions, while swinging from the ceiling, Colleen accidentally kicked Janice in the stomach. As punishment, Cameron took her sleeping bag from her box, so she had to sleep on the rough plasterboard. At the next torture session, he bought matches and burnt her breasts.

When Janice was away, Cameron would take Colleen to the shed for a special torture session, which would end with him wanting her to cuddle him. He said she could ask him anything she liked. It was over a year that she had any opportunity for conversation. She asked when he first realized that he wanted to hurt women. He said when he was five or six years old he had begun to draw pictures of women in bondage. Then she asked what he would do if someone did what he was doing to his daughter. Kill them, he said. So how did he think her father felt about what he was doing to her? That was the end of the conversation and she was returned to her box. On a hot summer day, it was unbearably stuffy in there. For once, she was grateful to be naked.

Colleen was in the box when Janice gave birth to her second daughter on the bed above. And she was in there for another Christmas, her 22nd birthday, and then New Year.

With another mouth to feed, Colleen's meagre rations were cut and Janice got an evening job. Cameron used her absence to rape Colleen, although she had to be tied up first and he would make the sex as rough and painful as possible. Sometimes he would suspend Colleen naked from the frame while he sat and watched TV. At weekends, Janice would join him while Colleen hung there in agony.

Seeking new diversions, despite her poor condition, Cameron would force her to run down isolated dirt roads, threatening to drag her behind the car with a chain around her neck if she would not. Or he would make her strip off and swim around a lake. He even did this with the children in the car.

From the trailer, she was to run time circuits; he said it would be reported to The Company if she was not back on time. There was no point in running to the neighbours; she assumed they were all tied up in The Company. They would have known she was a slave because she had a slave collar on – a new tight one that Cameron had soldered closed. When one neighbour tried to stop her for a chat, she ran on fearing that she would be reported.

More manual work was found for her and she was set to work making macramé plant holders at night, chained to the back of the toilet. For any perceived mistake, a new punishment was devised. She was suspended from the frame with her feet off the ground. Wires were taped to her breasts and the insides of her thighs, so Cameron could administer electric shocks while he and his wife watched TV with the volume up to drown out her screams. Afterwards, Colleen found that her flesh had been burned where the wires had been taped to her.

Cameron then built a new T-shaped frame. Blindfolded and naked, her arms were strapped to the crossbar of the T, her ankles to the foot. With a wrench, he turned a mechanism in the trunk of the T, lengthening it. Then he ran his hands up and down her body to feel the tension in her flesh. The pain was excruciating and he kept turning the mechanism until she passed out. When she came to, she had to beg for mercy. Then he raped her both orally and vaginally. Then he began turning the mechanism again with all his might. She thought that this would have killed her if one of the straps had not broken under the strain. She was left with a dislocated shoulder which she knocked back into place by hitting her arm against the side of the box. On another occasion, she was forced to perform cunnilingus on Janice. She was returned to her box. The couple then had sex with Colleen dry heaving beneath them.

Cameron got a job cutting cedar fence posts. He took Colleen with him. The other men were all with The

Company and he pointed out one man with a beard who, he said, was particularly hard on women slaves. On the way home in the pickup, Cameron ordered her to remove her trousers and masturbate with the handle of his whip.

As the slave collar round her neck was inviting questions, Cameron removed it. But, he said, The Company insisted that she have some slave identification so, without an anaesthetic, pierced her labia and put a ring in it.

Cameron forced Colleen to dig a hole under one of the storage sheds and lined it with bricks. When it was completed, this dungeon would be her new home. Later, it accommodated four of five other slaves and, as senior slave, he said, she would have to torture the new girls into submission.

That December, to her surprise, the Hookers asked Colleen what she wanted for Christmas. She said a Bible. She got it on 11 January. It was inscribed, 'A gift to Kay Powers from Cameron and Jan.' After that, she was allowed to spend her evenings reading it, chained to the toilet.

Short of money, Cameron took her panhandling. This brought her to the attention of a police officer who told her to move on. Terrified that the encounter may have been witnessed by The Company, she ran back to Cameron.

Both the Hookers took day jobs and Colleen was left to look after the kids. But she did not take the opportunity to call her parents or the police, fearing that The Company had the phone tapped.

A trusted slave, she was moved out of her box and allowed to sleep in the back bathroom, still in chains. One morning, one of the Hookers' daughters found her there. After that, Cameron told Colleen to lock the bathroom door from the inside. Colleen began cooking for the whole family, although everything she did was criticized and she was frequently beaten. She was also allowed to eat on the floor beside the table, unless either of their parents came to dinner.

Janice brought work from her job for Colleen to complete overnight. But when they found that Janice's employer would not pay overtime, Colleen was registered as an employee. By then it had been three years since she had disappeared and her name on a company's records alerted no one.

To terrorize Colleen further, Cameron told her that two men from The Company were coming to test her loyalty, so she had better prepare herself for a pretty vicious torture session. On another occasion, he took her out into the forest and left her there naked all night in the cold.

Cameron enjoyed his power over her so much that he told her to write down all the things he had done to her since she had first been captured. This provided damning evidence at his trial.

Colleen learnt to flatter Cameron, even writing him love letters. As a result, the torture was less frequent and less severe. The following summer, she was even allowed to talk to the neighbours, providing the conversation was confined to gardening. Anything else would result in a beating and a return to the box. From under the bed, Colleen could hear Cameron beating his wife. Once Cameron told Colleen to take the children outside so he could whip Janice. Afterwards, the girls wanted to know why Mommy was crying.

Plainly, the situation was falling apart. One day, Janice

gave Colleen new clothes and helped her with her make-up. In a bar, the two women picked up two guys and went back to their apartment. Janice disappeared into a bedroom with one of them.

There were other dates and family outings. On one of them, Colleen asked if she could phone her father in Riverside, California. At the payphone in a gas station, Cameron stood next to Colleen with his finger poised, ready to cut her off. The phone was answered by Colleen's sister Bonnie. Colleen explained that she had been staying with friends. After five minutes, Cameron indicated that Colleen should end the conversation and she put the phone down. She was also allowed to write home. Cameron vetted the letters and they were posted from nearby towns with no return address. And there were more calls.

After two years' work, the dungeon under the storage shed was finished. Through a trapdoor in the floor of the shed, Colleen descended a ladder. The dungeon was deep, so the ceiling high enough for her to be hung up. It was furnished with her sleeping bag, a chair, her Bible and a portable radio. Once Colleen was in the dungeon, Cameron hauled up the ladder and closed the trap door. But when it rained, the dungeon filled with water and Colleen was returned to the box.

The situation in the trailer grew worse when Janice found Colleen's diary, which enumerated her many rapes. In it, Colleen also wrote flatteringly of her 'love' for Cameron. Then the Hookers' older daughter inadvertently called Colleen 'Mom'. Cameron took Colleen out to the forest, tied her between two trees, and whipped her.

In March, with Colleen kneeling with her head bowed

before her Master, she was told The Company had decided to let her visit her family. Their houses were bugged, she was told. Any hint of disloyalty and the house would be swamped by security. But first she had to be hung up and whipped. This was to be done at a small farm Cameron's father had in Oregon. There, she was hung up naked in the barn and when his father walked in, Cameron quickly let her down. But it was dark in the barn and she could not be sure what the old man had seen.

On the day Cameron was supposed to take her to the bus station for her trip home, he simply drove her around, then returned to the trailer and put her back in the box. More savage beatings followed. As a final test, Cameron said, she was to put a shotgun in her mouth and pull the trigger. She did it without hesitation. The hammer came down on an empty chamber and she had passed the test.

On 20 March 1981, Cameron set off up Interstate 5 with Colleen in the car. As they neared Sacramento, he said he wanted to check in with The Company's headquarters there. He left her in the car for 15 minutes while he disappeared into an anonymous building.

At Riverside, Cameron dropped Colleen outside her grandmother's house. After a quick visit, he drove her to her father's place. He dropped her there and drove away. Her stepmother and sisters were there and her mother, who lived nearby, turned up later. Naturally, they wanted to know where she had been for the past four years, but they did not want to put too much pressure on her in case they pushed her away for ever. They assumed that she had joined some weird cult. Long before, the police had written her off as a runaway.

The next day, she went to church with her grandmother. After a family lunch, Cameron arrived to collect her. He introduced himself as Mike and said that he was Colleen's fiancé. He said he was just moving house, so he could not give them a phone number.

Arriving back at the trailer the following morning, they found that Janice and the kids were staying with her family. So Colleen was then raped and returned to the box. For the next three years, she was allowed out of the box once the children had gone to bed; sometimes she was not released at all. She ate only four or five times a week and her weight declined dramatically. Kept constantly in the dark, her hair began to fall out and her bones became brittle. When she was trussed up in the torture frame, part of her big toe came away. Cameron was furious that she had bled on the carpet.

That summer, when Cameron and the family went away for three days, Colleen was left in the box with a quart of water and a pack of cookies while the temperature in Red Bluff soared above 120°F. When the family returned, Colleen was too weak to stand up.

Whenever Janice and the children were out, the torturing, beating and raping continued. All the while, Cameron thought up fresh horrors; he would tie her calves to her thighs until she lost all feeling in her legs. Then he would put a rubber gas mask over her head; the eyes were taped over and only one tiny air hole was left open. Cameron would put his finger over it until she was on the verge of suffocating.

In October 1983, she was transferred back to the dungeon under the shed. There she could read the Bible and listen to a Christian station on the radio. But when one of the children peeped inside, she was returned to the box. Meanwhile, Janice had begun to take an interest in the Bible, too, and she and Colleen began to study it together.

On her 27th birthday, Colleen was given a birthday cake. Then she was re-introduced to the Hookers' daughters who had not seen her for three years. It was time for Colleen to bring money into the household again. On 21 May 1984, Janice drove her to Red Bluff where she found a job as a housekeeper at a motel only a few hundred yards from where she had been picked up seven years earlier. She was still too afraid of The Company to go to the Red Bluff Police Department nearby.

Janice and Colleen went to church together; the pastor even visited them at the trailer. When Cameron suggested that he make Colleen his second wife, Janice initially acquiesced. Then, one day, she turned up at the motel and told Colleen that Cameron was not a member of The Company; the whole thing had been made up. Colleen could hardly believe her ears. She broke down. For seven years, she had been a prisoner of his lies.

They went to the pastor and told him everything, but it was too late to make off with the kids that night, so they had to go back to the trailer and pretend nothing had changed.

In the morning, after Cameron had gone to work, they fled to Janice's parents' house. Colleen's father wired her the bus fare home. The next morning, as Janice drove Colleen to the bus station, she begged her not to go to the police.

Arriving in Riverside, Colleen told her family of her 2,634 days of captivity, although she spared them the most painful details. She then discovered that her family had made every effort to find her. They had even visited Red Bluff, but she had simply vanished into thin air.

Over the next few months, Janice and Colleen exchanged calls. Even Cameron phoned. After Colleen had left, Janice had returned to Cameron, who promised to reform. He burnt his bondage gear, his collection of pornography and the pictures he had taken of Colleen being tortured, and went into counselling with the pastor. But Janice was not convinced that he had changed. Afraid for her children, she told the pastor to call the police.

Soon afterwards, Colleen received a call from Red Bluff Police Department. They visited her in Riverside and took pictures of her scars. Colleen's story matched with what Janice had told them – except for something that Colleen could not have known. There had indeed been another victim. Over a year before Colleen had been kidnapped, the Hookers had picked up a girl named Marie Elizabeth 'Marliz' Spannhake. But in the basement, she would not stop screaming. So Cameron got a kitchen knife and cut her vocal cords. As he could not staunch the bleeding, he killed her with his bare hands and buried her in a shallow grave. Marliz was the girl whose picture Colleen had seen in the box under the Hookers' bed.

Even with Janice's help, the police could not find her body, so they did not charge Cameron with murder. Instead, he was charged with the kidnapping, seven counts of rape, three counts of false imprisonment, two counts of abduction to live in an illicit relationship, one forced oral copulation, one sodomy, and one penetration with a foreign object – the whip handle.

A thorough medical examination documented the

electrical burns on Colleen's body, the scarring from straps and whips, the damage to her shoulder from stretching, the inexpertly pierced labia and her general poor state of health from years of malnutrition and confinement. Everything backed up her story.

Meanwhile, Colleen's home was besieged by the media, who were calling her 'The Girl in the Box'. She moved out to live with a new boyfriend and, eager to return to normal life, she got a job in a store. But there was still the trial to go through.

Cameron pleaded not guilty to all charges. As this was not a murder case and the state of California was short of funds, the DA was forced to plea bargain. But when it appeared that Cameron might serve less time in captivity than Colleen had, there was such a furore that funds were allocated and the plea bargain was dropped.

At the Superior Court of California, the defence argued that the statute of limitations had run out on the 1977 kidnapping and, after that, she was a 'willing participant'. The prosecution countered that the kidnapping had been continuous up until 1984 when she escaped.

The box and many of the instruments with which Cameron had used to torture Colleen were brought into the court, but the defence would argue that these were used in a consensual relationship between two adults and no laws had been broken. On the stand, Janice outlined her bizarre relationship with Cameron and detailed his aberrant sexual interests. Her husband was dyslexic, she said, and she had read him articles on the techniques of brainwashing that he had then employed on Colleen. She had also found the slave contract that Colleen had been forced to sign. She told the court about The Company. Cameron, she said, had promised not to have sex with his slave girl and went along with it to see how far he would go. When she started raping her, she fled. However, she did admit whipping Colleen while her husband watched and fuelling his fantasies by reading S&M magazines to him.

Colleen's confinement in the box was sometimes due to Janice's jealousy. But Janice said Cameron continued torturing her, too. She was only spared the electric shocks and the box. She maintained that, like Colleen, she was one of Cameron's victims, not his accomplice.

Colleen found it intimidating to testify in the courtroom just a few feet from Cameron. She was also afraid that he might be acquitted. The defence maintained that, after the initial abduction, the relationship had been consensual. She had written Cameron love letters. Colleen insisted that she had done that so he would not hurt her. During her first six months alone, he had hung her up naked 90 or 100 times and whipped her savagely. It took her three-and-a-half days on the stand to detail the barbarity that he had inflicted on her. But the most damning evidence were the pictures of both Janice and Colleen being hung up.

Taking the stand, Cameron Hooker said that he had long been fascinated with bondage, discipline, sadism and masochism. Between consenting adults, these things were legal and Janice shared his interests. Many other people were willing to become slaves. He claimed that, when they gave Colleen a lift, she appeared to be spaced out on illegal drugs. He admitted the initial kidnapping. It was for her own good, but as the statute of limitations had run out he could not be charged with that.

He held her while she was going through her withdrawal symptoms and he only put her in a crate with a box over her head, not as torture, but to keep her quiet. After she had been with them for about three months, she, too, became interested in bondage. Then Colleen kept asking him for sex, but he had promised Janice that he would not. It was Janice who found the slave contract and she came up with the story about the all-powerful Company which might intimidate Colleen so much that they would be able to let her go. Then, once the contract was signed, Janice began to treat Colleen like a slave.

When Janice fell pregnant a second time, she went off sex. To arouse Janice, Colleen agreed to be tied up spread-eagled on the bed. He maintained that he was kissing Janice while touching Colleen. However, Janice was not turned on, so he began having sex with Colleen, but Janice could not handle it, so Colleen was returned, disappointed, to the basement. He then claimed that they decided to release Colleen by pretending that they were buying her freedom from The Company. She was told that she could leave but, if she went to the police, The Company would punish her. But first she helped them move into their mobile home.

During the move, she slept in a box or in the bathroom, and was not restrained. She volunteered to become their slave and did not try to escape. She helped dig a trench to install the utilities and worked with him cutting fence posts. He admitted tying her to a tree, but they spent time talking and kissing. He told her that, when they released her, she must never talk about The Company, or The Company would make her someone else's slave. He never threatened her family, he said.

SLAVE IN A BOX

While Cameron claimed that he treated Colleen well, he said Janice treated her cruelly like a slave. He offered to take Colleen back to her family, but she said that her family was abusive and she did not want to go back to taking drugs. She said she would rather stay where she was and have the stability of a loving family around her.

While Colleen was happy to stay as a slave, Cameron said, Janice wanted her to go because she was afraid that he and Colleen were falling in love. She was the one who punished Colleen. True, he hung Colleen up, but when he went to look for more straps, he came back to find Janice administering electric shocks.

His relationship with Colleen was affectionate. They began having sex, although the bondage continued. Colleen cried when he put her on the stretcher, but she could take more pain than he could dish out, he maintained. They dug the dungeon under the shed because, with the children growing older, they could not continue their bondage sessions in the trailer. Colleen helped in its construction; the whips were merely toys. They were not meant to hurt anyone. After Janice was kicked in the stomach, it was Janice who went to get the matches and burnt Colleen's breasts, he maintained.

The sex continued when Janice went out to work, at Colleen's instigation. She wanted to get married and have his baby. By then Janice was seeing other men. But this did not upset him as he was in love with Colleen. They took her out shopping and on outings, and he bought her a Bible. As he was a poor reader, she read out passages to him.

At Colleen's home, Cameron had introduced himself as 'Mike' and did not give them his phone number because he did not want another set of troublesome in-laws. Colleen voluntarily returned to Red Bluff with him because she loved him. And she returned to her box to save his marriage. Janice would have left him otherwise.

When the problems in his marriage had been ironed out, Colleen came out of the box again. She and Janice then grew friendly and, he maintained, began having lesbian sex together. Colleen then wanted to go out to work and voluntarily contributed most of her wages to the household finances. The idea of Colleen becoming his second wife came from their reading the Bible – Abraham took the slave girl Hagar as his second wife after Sarah proved barren.

Once Colleen discovered that The Company was not real, she said that she was going back to her family because she did not want to come between him and Janice. After she arrived home, she even phoned to tell him she loved him. Then she began bombarding him with letters and phone calls. This upset Janice. He maintained that they had had the perfect love triangle. But, in the end, the two women ganged up on him and had him arrested, so that they could resume their lesbian relationship.

Both Janice and Colleen participated willingly in bondage, Cameron said. After the initial abduction, he never held her against her will. She could have left at any time; she was seen out jogging and went out on dates with other men – and he never raped her. All the sex was consensual. She loved him; her letters proved that. It was only when he found himself the unwanted corner of a love triangle that they decided to get rid of him by sending him to prison.

Cameron's family and friends then testified that they had

seen 'Kay' on numerous occasions. As their housekeeper and babysitter, she was very much part of the family and never protested in any way.

The defence then called a psychiatrist who had testified in the trial of Patty Hearst to challenge the prosecution's allegation that Colleen had been brainwashed. He said that, although she may have been coerced during the first six months of her captivity, after that, she participated willingly. Consequently, the prosecution dropped the charges of false imprisonment and abduction to live in an illicit relationship. However, the jury still had a roster of charges to consider. It took them two-and-a-half days to find Cameron Hooker guilty on all the other counts, except one last rape, where the jury was divided. The reasoning seems to have been that, after seven years of savage abuse, Colleen may have tacitly accepted her tormentor's advances.

Sentencing Cameron to 104 years in jail, the judge said, 'I consider the defendant the most dangerous psychopath I have ever dealt with, in that he is the opposite of what he seems. He will be a danger to women as long as he is alive.'

Given time off for good behaviour, Cameron will be eligible for parole in 2023, when he is 70. However, by that time, the body of Marliz Spannhake might have been found and he would then face a murder charge.

PART III
INTERNATIONAL
ABDUCTION

17

THE FATHER
FROM HELL

Internationally, the most shocking case of sexual slavery was that of Elisabeth Fritzl. She had been held in a basement dungeon under her family home in Austria for 14 years and been repeatedly raped and sexually abused by her own father. When she emerged in April 2008, she brought with her three children sired by her father who had spent their whole lives in the dungeon. Another had died and the body had been disposed of in a furnace. Three more had been cared for upstairs by their grandparents.

The family home was at 40 Ybbsstrasse in the small town of Amstetten in Austria, some 30 miles from the Czech border. During the Cold War, this was the front line. Eighteen-year-old Elisabeth Fritzl had disappeared on the night of 28 August 1984. Elisabeth was woken by her father, who asked her to come down to the cellar with him; he had been building a nuclear air-raid shelter down there. It was a strange request, but her father was a severe and demanding parent, and it was best to do what he said. He wanted her to help grapple a heavy steel door into place. That done, he grabbed her from behind and knocked her out with ether. When she awoke, she found herself in total darkness, handcuffed to a metal pole. The basement bunker was not intended to be an air-raid shelter, but a prison.

The dungeon was insulated and soundproofed and Elisabeth could scream herself hoarse. No one could hear her. The people in the town were told that she had run off to join a religious sect. This was not hard to believe; she had tried to escape from her abusive dad before.

After a couple of days, Elisabeth was released from the handcuffs and put on a long leash so she could reach a makeshift lavatory. Then her father started raping her. But he had already been sexually abusing her throughout her childhood. There was little point in putting up any resistance. 'I faced the choice of being left to starve or being raped,' she said. She faced the same choice for the next 8,516 days.

When Josef Fritzl was finally brought to book, he made no attempt to explain the incarceration and rape of his daughter. He has claimed to be a victim of Austria's Nazi past. Born in 1935, he was nearly three when the people of Amstetten lined the road with the arms raised to greet Hitler – himself an Austrian by birth – as he drove into Austria in 1938 to annex the country as part of Greater Germany. After the 1938 *Anschluss*, Hitler was made an honorary citizen of Amstetten.

When Fritzl's mother threw his father out of the house, he had no further contact with him. After a scandalous divorce, his father was killed in the war. After Hitler invaded the Soviet Union in 1941, Germany used the rail line through Amstetten to move men and munitions to the front; it was repeatedly bombed by Allies. Consequently, Fritzl spent much of his childhood taking shelter in the cellar.

In town, there was a camp for the slave labourers who rebuilt the railway after the bombing raids, along with a concentration camp for women. Inmates of the nearby Mauer clinic, where Elisabeth and her children would recuperate after their ordeal, were exterminated in the Nazi euthanasia programme.

By the age of ten, Fritzl would have been a member of the Hitler Youth. It was compulsory. Indeed, in the cellar of his home in Ybbsstrasse, he called himself the '*Führer*' – and he was the master of his own warped 'Reich'. 'I grew up in the Nazi era and strictness and discipline were very important then,' he said. In the post-war Soviet occupation of Austria, local women were regularly raped by Russian soldiers. Times were hard and Fritzl's mother was strict, often beating hims.

At school, he was a loner. He went to college to study electrical engineering and took an apprenticeship at a steel works. At 21, he met 17-year-old Rosemarie, who became his wife. She gave him seven children – two sons and five daughters.

At 24, Fritzl came to the attention of the police for exposing himself. He raped at least two women in Linz, though only one pressed charges. He was jailed for 18 months. But he was a talented engineer and quickly found a new job when he was released and soon became a pillar of the community.

He invested in property, including a guesthouse and

camping ground on the shores of Lake Mondsee near Salzburg. And he extended the house in Ybbsstrasse to take in tenants. They lived directly over the cellar that Fritzl also extended under the back garden.

He was a strict father; his sister-in-law compared him to a drill sergeant. The children called him a tyrant and married young to leave home. However, one son had learning difficulties. He remained at home and Fritzl used him as a skivvy. The other son told a friend that he was afraid his father might kill him. As the prettiest of Fritzl's daughters, Elisabeth was his favourite, but he brutalized her, too. A shy child, she was never seen to laugh. She took care to hide the bruises on her body from her schoolfriends.

Fritzl also beat his wife, and mocked and humiliated her in public. In 1973, she moved to the guesthouse at Mondsee, but Fritzl insisted that the children stay with him at Ybbsstrasse. Soon, she moved back home again. The guesthouse had burned down. Fritzl was charged with arson, but acquitted due to lack of evidence.

He began abusing Elisabeth aged 11 while her mother and the other children were on holiday. Afterwards, he was brutally strict with her in public but, when they were alone, he'd rape her without warning – in his car, on walks in the woods, even in the cellar, Elisabeth said.

Fritzl denied this. 'I am not a man who would molest children,' he said. 'I only had sex with her later, much later.' But Elisabeth asserts that it began much earlier and there is circumstantial evidence to support her accusations. Elisabeth had to be home half-an-hour after school finished and she was terrified of being late. Friends who accompanied her would disappear when her father showed up. She was not allowed out in the evening or to invite friends to the house.

As she approached adolescence, Fritzl grew increasingly possessive. He flew into a rage if she tried to dress fashionably, wore make-up or mentioned boys. Friends were banned from the house and she became sullen and withdrawn. All the time, Fritzl was making plans.

Elisabeth was just 12 in 1978 when Fritzl applied for planning permission to turn his basement into a nuclear shelter. This was not uncommon in Austria at the time. Over the next six years, he turned the bunker into an unbreachable fortress. In 1983, building inspectors gave their approval to the alterations. Elisabeth was then 15.

The following year, 16-year-old Elisabeth ran away from home. She found work as a waitress, but the police found out where she was and brought her back. But when she was 18, they would not be able to do that; she already had a bag packed. So when she then disappeared, no one was surprised. Her friends were happy that she had escaped at last, while to the older generation she was an ungrateful child who had gone off the rails.

In the cellar, Fritzl could do what he pleased. He had been planning this for six long years. At first, he beat her to get his way. Soon, she realized that there was no point in fighting him. The beatings lessened, but not the demand for sex. For the first nine months, she was kept on a leash. She lost count of how many times she was raped during that time. Fritzl also denied this. 'We first had sex in spring 1985 ...' – at least six months after he imprisoned her, he claimed.

Once he had imprisoned her and had her completely in his power, his desire for her became irresistible, he said. 'I could not control myself any more. I wanted to have children with her. It was my dream to have another normal family, in the cellar, with her as a good wife and several children ... At some stage, somewhere in the night, I went into the cellar. I knew that Elisabeth did not want it, what I did with her. The pressure to do the forbidden thing was just too big to withstand.'

According to Fritzl, Elisabeth did not resist, although she cried quietly afterwards. After that, every two or three days, he would go into the cellar to bring her food and a change of clothes, then have sex with her. He also beat her for the sadistic pleasure of it. Increasingly, he said, sex with his daughter became 'an obsession'.

Again, he was unrepentant. 'Why should I be sorry?' he said. 'I took good care of her. I saved her from falling into the drug scene.' Yet there is no indication that Elisabeth Fritzl ever took drugs or was interested in doing so.

The day after her daughter disappeared, Rosemarie Fritzl went to the police and reported her as missing. To allay suspicion, Fritzl forced Elisabeth to write a letter, saying that she was staying with a friend and warning her parents not to look for her, otherwise she would flee the country. It was dated 21 September 1984 and was postmarked Braunau am Inn, Hitler's birthplace. Fritzl handed it over to the police. As Elisabeth was no longer a minor, they had no obligation to look for her. Case closed.

Fritzl forced Elisabeth to write other letters to her mother. In them, she was to pretend she had joined a religious sect. No one questioned this or asked whether such sects operated in Austria – they don't. Religious groups that isolate members from their family and friends are practically unknown outside Japan and the English-speaking world.

Within the family, Fritzl would brook no enquiry. Rosemarie was browbeaten. Other members of the family dared not challenge him. To acquaintances, he made great play of being a concerned parent and claimed that Interpol were still looking for her.

Below street level, Fritzl kept up a sickening pretence of normality with his daughter. He would tell her how work on the garden above her was progressing and keep her updated on the progress of her brothers and sisters. He crowed that everyone had fallen for the lies he had told. For her, there was no hope of rescue. After all, the very last place anyone would have looked for her was in her own home.

Elisabeth now had to cope with the full force of Fritzl's libido as he had stopped sleeping with Rosemarie. 'You're too fat for sex,' he told his wife in front of family and friends. 'Fat women are below my standard.' To a friend, he boasted of having girlfriend – a thin one. The friend never guessed that Fritzl was talking about his daughter.

For the first four years, he kept Elisabeth in complete isolation – then she fell pregnant. Any hope that he may release her so she could have the child under medical supervision was dashed when he bought her a medical book. She was going to have to manage on her own.

Fritzl drove hundreds of miles to places no one would recognize him to buy baby food, clothes and Pampers. Then he left his terrified 22-year-old daughter to give birth to her daughter, Kerstin, in the cellar alone. Miraculously, both mother and child survived. Elisabeth was no longer alone in her dungeon. On the other hand, Kerstin was living, breathing proof of what he had done. Now he would never be able to let her go.

Kerstin was sickly from the time she was born. She suffered from a form of epilepsy that is linked to incest, but she was denied any medical attention. Fritzl was happy with the child; there were fewer beatings, although the rapes soon resumed. He even brought Elizabeth new clothes – largely lingerie and provocative outfits for his own benefit, naturally.

The following year, she gave birth to a son – Stefan. The three of them were living in one small bedsit with a floor space of 215sq ft (20sq m) where Fritzl was having sex with his daughter in front of their children, which must only have added to her distress. And in terms of proximity to others, Elisabeth and her burgeoning family were only a few feet from the lodgers who were living upstairs. One of them, Joseph Leitner, had known Elisabeth as a girl and even knew that her father had raped her. But he, too, swallowed the story that she had run off to join a sect.

Despite Fritzl's ban on pets, Leitner kept a dog that barked every time anyone passed the cellar door. But Fritzl warned all his tenants that the cellar was strictly off-limits. Leitner also noticed that his electricity bill was exorbitant. With all the appliances in his room unplugged, the electricity meter still spun round at high speed. It seems that Fritzl was tapping electricity from his one-room apartment into the cellar below. Before Leitner could complain, Fritzl spotted his dog and threw him out.

Another tenant, Alfred Dubanovsky, had been a friend of Elisabeth's at school; he also knew of her abusive home life. For 12 years, he lived a few feet above her head. At night, he saw Fritzl taking food down to the cellar in a wheelbarrow, but he never imagined that anyone was living down there. Other tenants noticed food missing. Fritzl, it seems, stole from his lodgers to feed his captives.

Fritzl's own visits to the basement seemed to others innocuous enough. He went down there ostensibly to do some work on some electrical engineering plans in a makeshift office. Rosemarie had been told never to disturb him while he was at work and sometimes he slipped down there after she had gone to bed. None of the neighbours would have noticed anything suspicious – the entrance to the cellar was in the back garden and was hidden by a tall hedge.

In 1992, Elisabeth gave birth to a second daughter, Lisa. She had a heart defect caused by her incestuous parentage and cried a lot. Fritzl was afraid that someone may hear her and decided that the child should be taken upstairs where she could receive proper medical attention. All Elisabeth had to do was write another letter, saying, 'Dear parents, You will probably be shocked to hear from me after all these years, and with a real-life surprise, no less ... I am leaving you my little daughter Lisa. Take good care of my little girl.' She went on to say that the sect had no time for children and begged her parents to bring her child up for her.

On 19 May 1993, Lisa duly appeared on the Fritzls' front doorstep in a cardboard box with the letter attached. At first, Rosemarie was sceptical, but Fritzl coerced his daughter into taping a telephone message. To complete the illusion, Fritzl got the police to confirm that the letter came from Elisabeth by asking a handwriting expert to compare it with the writing in her old exercise books. Curiously, the social services did not even ask why a woman would entrust her child to parents she, herself, had run away from, and the

Fritzls were allowed to adopt their grandchild. This went ahead even though Fritzl had a conviction for rape. In Austria, criminal records are expunged after ten years.

While Lisa flourished in the light and fresh air upstairs, it was only a matter of time before Elisabeth fell pregnant again. To accommodate more captives, the cellar would have to be extended. Elisabeth was set the task of digging out over 4,000cu ft (116cu m) of earth – 200 tons of it – by hand. Over the next few years, Fritzl managed to move the equivalent of 17 lorryloads out of the cellar without anyone noticing. At the same time, he moved in tiles, bricks, wooden wall panels, a washing machine, a kitchen sink, beds and pipework without anybody being any the wiser.

The dungeon ended up seven times the size of the nuclear bunker he had sought permission to construct. On top of all his other crimes, Fritzl had violated every building code, but the authorities took no notice. Even more horrifying, while all this was going on, Elisabeth, Kerstin and Stefan had to survive amid the dirt of the excavation and construction work.

While the subterranean family had more room, there was no more light or air. Elisabeth cajoled Fritzl into installing a UV light and supplying vitamin D tablets to compensate partially for the lack of sunlight. But he would not extend the ventilation system; this would risk sound getting out. The last thing he wanted was Elisabeth being able to summon help. As the children grew older, the air grew so stale that they had to spend most of their time sitting down. And despite the extensive evacuations, the ceiling was never more than 5ft 6in (1.7 m) high. In some places, the ceiling was a good deal lower. Elisabeth and the children, as they grew, had to stoop. And now with a shower in the cellar, the atmosphere was damp.

On 26 February 1994, Elisabeth gave birth to her fourth child – Monika. But the extension of the cellar was far from complete, so Fritzl repeated the charade he went through with Lisa, and Monika turned up on the doorstep on 16 December. This time, the phone call came through on the Fritzls' new, unlisted number. Even this did not alert the authorities. The Fritzls did not adopt Monika; by fostering her, they received a state benefit of €400 (£340) a month.

Two years later, Elisabeth gave birth to twins. This must have been doubly frightening as, with no ultrasound scan, she would not have known she was carrying two babies. One of them had breathing difficulties and, when Fritzl returned to the cellar three days later, the little boy was dead. Fritzl burnt the body in the basement furnace along with other household waste. The surviving twin, Alexander, went upstairs and was passed off as another foundling. Again, the authorities failed to investigate and Fritzl benefited from another foster fee.

Over the years, the social services paid at least 21 visits and noted that the children were doing well. While Fritzl was strict, neighbours and their school reported that the children were happy and well adjusted. They had just one fear – that their mother might return and reclaim them.

Some of Fritzl's business deals did not go well and he was now short of money. Two small fires in the house brought in cash from insurance claims. Despite the previous arson charges, there was little more than a cursory investigation. But if one of the fires had got out of control, there would have been no hope for the captives in the dungeon below.

When Kerstin and Stefan grew to maturity, Fritzl found himself keeping three adults in the cellar. But they were too weak to overpower him. Anyway, there was no escape. To open the door, you needed a security code. Fritzl said that whoever touched the door would be electrocuted and he would pump poison gas into the cellar at the slightest hint of rebellion. He claimed that a timing mechanism would open the door if he died on the outside or if an accident prevented him returning. Nothing of that nature was found. Nevertheless, Fritzl treated himself to long holidays in Thailand where he was a sex tourist, and he paid regular visits to a brothel in Linz where he paid to have sex in the brothel's dungeon.

One of the prostitutes said, 'He chose me because he said he liked young, plump girls who were happy to submit to him.' Others were frightened by his sadistic demands. He was also seen in S&M clubs where he would feed himself up on Viagra and other performance-enhancing drugs. None of this seemed to lessen his rapacious sexual demands when he returned to the cellar in Ybbsstrasse.

In 2003, Elisabeth gave birth to her seventh child, a boy she named Felix. The extension of the cellar was now complete and Felix was going remain in the dungeon. At 63, Fritzl thought Rosemarie was too old to bring up another child. The upstairs children received a normal education, but in the dungeon Elisabeth taught the children as best she could. Only a small television, which Fritzl eventually provided, gave the children some impression of what the world outside was like. But it was difficult to impose any structure on their lives when it was impossible to tell day from night.

Fritzl claimed that he did his best for his second family in the basement. He provided a cooker and a freezer so that they would have fresh food while he was away in Thailand. In 2002, he bought Elisabeth a washing machine. Until then, she had had to wash everything by hand. He brought a tree down to them at Christmas and celebrated their birthdays. But instead of cheap presents, they needed light, air and freedom.

In a grotesque parody of home life, he watched videos with the children while Elisabeth cooked dinner. He even showed them some footage he had shot of their brothers and sisters upstairs, so the downstairs brood could see what they were missing. He also played pornographic videos and forced Elisabeth to re-enact scenes with him.

Fritzl saw nothing wrong in this and claimed to have loved his family in the cellar. They accepted him as the head of the family and Elisabeth stayed strong. 'She never complained,' he said, 'even when her teeth slowly went rotten and fell out of her mouth one by one, and she suffered day and night with unbearable pain and could not sleep. She stayed strong for the children. But the children ... I saw they were constantly getting weaker.' But he did nothing about it.

Due to the fetid air, the children suffered from respiratory problems. Both Felix and Kerstin were wracked with coughing fits and uncontrollable convulsions. Felix would shake for hours on end, while Kerstin would scream hysterically. Elisabeth had to treat them as best she could with the rudimentary store-bought medicines – aspirin, cough mixture and the like – that Fritzl provided. They never saw a doctor and the children had none of the regular inoculations given in infancy. It is a miracle they survived at all.

In 2005, Fritzl celebrated his 70th birthday party in the garden above. The following year, the mayor of Amstetten hosted a reception for the Fritzls' 50th wedding anniversary.

With Elisabeth toothless and ageing, Fritzl no longer found her sexually attractive. There were allegations that he turned his attentions to Kerstin. But he, too, was growing old and it was clear that the situation could not go on indefinitely. Towards the end of 2007, Fritzl began preparing an exit strategy. His plan was, the following summer, for Elisabeth to quit the obscure sect that had held her for the past quarter of a century and return home. The shocking physical condition of her and her children would be blamed on their maltreatment inflicted on them by the cult.

At Christmas, Fritzl got Elisabeth to write a letter, telling her parents that she was quitting the sect and would be home in six months 'if all goes well'. But then Kerstin fell dangerously ill. Spewing blood from her mouth, she lapsed into a coma. If something was not done urgently, it was clear that she would die.

Rosemarie was on holiday in Italy with the children, so one night Fritzl and Elisabeth carried the unconscious 19-year-old up into the house above. Elisabeth then had to return to the dungeon as the other two boys were still down there. Fritzl called an ambulance. At 7.00am on Saturday, 19 April 2008, the wan, ghostlike Kerstin Fritzl was admitted to hospital where the staff had no idea what to make of her. An hour later, Fritzl turned up. He told them, once again, that his daughter had run off to join some mysterious religious sect and had dumped another of her children on his doorstep. The note that came with her said, 'Wednesday, I gave her aspirin and cough medicine for the condition. Thursday, the cough worsened. Friday, the coughing gets even worse. She has been biting her lip as well as her tongue. Please, please help her! Kerstin is really terrified of other people, she was never in a hospital. If there are any problems please ask my father for help, he is the only person that she knows.' A postscript was addressed to the stricken girl herself: 'Kerstin – please stay strong, until we see each other again! We will come back to you soon!'

Dr Albert Reiter was on duty in the emergency room that morning. He did not believe that a mother who had written such a note would abandon her daughter in such a state. He was suspicious of the child's deathly pallor, which did not seem to have anything to do with the disease she was suffering from. And it was puzzling that such a young person should have lost all their teeth.

Kerstin was at death's door. Her entire immune system had collapsed and she was kept alive by a ventilator and a kidney dialysis machine. Even specialists called in from Vienna were of little help. To have any chance of saving her, they would need to know something of her medical history, so Dr Reiter issued an appeal for her mother to come forward.

The police were called in to check with general practitioners; none had any record of her. They, too, wanted to interview the girl's mother over possible criminal charges concerning her daughter's neglect.

Elisabeth saw Dr Reiter's appeal on TV and she begged her father to let her go to the hospital. She promised not to give him away and would maintain the fiction that she had been with a religious sect – just as she had promised to do that coming summer.

On Saturday, 26 April – one week after Kerstin had arrived in hospital – Elisabeth was let out of the cellar again. Fritzl called the hospital to tell Dr Reiter the good news – Elisabeth had returned and he was bringing her to the hospital. But when Elisabeth and Josef Fritzl arrived at the hospital, the police pounced. They arrested Elisabeth for child neglect, but Fritzl put up a fight – ostensibly to protect his daughter – so he was arrested, too.

At the station, the police could see immediately that there was something wrong with Elisabeth. She was only 42, but with her grey hair, no teeth and a morbidly pallid complexion she looked like a woman in her sixties. And, clearly, she was terrified. At first, she refused to answer their questions. Then she reverted to the script her father had prepared for her. She had run away to join a religious sect that had little time for children, so she had sent three of her children to her parents. But that did not explain the terrible condition of her daughter or her own appearance.

As the interrogation continued, Elisabeth grew agitated. Then she begged for assurances that neither she nor her children would ever have to see her father again. After the police agreed to this, she told them the harrowing story of her 24 years in captivity. They could not believe what they were hearing. Herr Fritzl was a pillar of the community, a respectable family man. However, Elisabeth's appearance and the shocking condition of her daughter was material evidence that what she was saying was true.

When Elisabeth's allegations were put to Fritzl, he refused to talk. But there was one way to find out if Elisabeth was telling the truth. They searched the house at 40 Ybbsstrasse. But the entrance to the dungeon was so well hidden they initially drew a blank.

Perhaps sensing that the game was up, Fritzl then led them through the five rooms in the basement. They went through his makeshift office and the boiler room where the dead child's body had been burnt. Along the way, they passed through eight locked doors. Behind a shelving unit in Fritzl's basement workshop was a heavy steel door just 3ft high with an electronic locking device. Fritzl gave the police the code to open it and they squeezed through.

Inside was a narrow corridor that led to a padded room. This was where Elisabeth had originally been confined and repeatedly abused. It was soundproofed with rubber cladding, so no scream, cry or sob could escape. Beyond it was a small living area. A passage so narrow that you had to turn sideways to get down it led to a rudimentary kitchen and bathroom, and two small bedrooms, each with two beds in them. The furnishings were sparse, lit by electric lightbulbs which went on and off on a timer. It was difficult to breathe.

In the midst of this pitiful scene, the police found what looked like two ashen-faced troglodytes. Nowhere could 18-year-old Stefan stand upright, while 5-year-old Felix preferred to go on all fours and had a strange simian gait. Both were pale, bent and terrified. Once outside, the two boys were overawed by daylight. It was something they had never seen before. They babbled in their own private language, but were able to communicate in German. Felix pointed at the sky and asked, 'Is God up there?'

As they were unused to sunlight, the police waited until

dusk to take them to hospital. All four of the captives were suffering from vitamin D deficiency, anaemia and malnutrition. Their immune systems had also been damaged and Felix's muscles and joints had failed to develop properly.

Kerstin pulled through and eventually joined the rest of the family – including the children who had been raised upstairs – at the Amstetten Mauer Landesklinikum psychiatric clinic where the entire family underwent therapy. Elisabeth and the children from the cellar were gradually introduced to sunlight and were expected to make a full recovery.

After DNA tests confirmed that Josef Fritzl was the father of all six surviving children, he was charged with rape, incest, coercion, false imprisonment, enslavement and negligent homicide. He pleaded guilty to all charges except enslavement and murder. However, after sitting through 11 hours of his daughter's videotape testimony, he changed his plea to guilty on enslavement and homicide as well. He was sentenced to life imprisonment and committed to an institution for the criminally insane. The minimum tariff was set at 15 years, but it is unlikely that he will ever be released.

18

THE BRITISH
FRITZL

In November 2008, there emerged in Sheffield a case that the newspapers referred to as 'the British Fritzl'. The defendant – referred to as 'Mr X' in court – remained anonymous to protect his daughters and their seven surviving children. Over 28 years, this father had raped his two daughters, making them pregnant 19 times. He then lived off the child benefit generated by the children they produced.

The father, who called himself 'The Gaffer', was a violent alcoholic. He beat his wife, who eventually left him. His children were terrorized from infancy. Before she was even six years old, the elder girl was seen by a health visitor with bruises after a beating from her father, and her younger sibling was found bruised at the age of two. He began sexually abusing his two daughters at the age of eight and ten. He beat them savagely to make them comply. It was said that he took pleasure in these sadistic assaults and only stopped beating them when they were pregnant. It was only then that the sisters realized that their father had been raping both of them.

'He started touching me when I was about five,' the elder daughter told the *Sun*. 'It was going on for years but I didn't know my younger sister was also being abused until much later.'

Suspicions were first raised in 1976. Sheffield social services remained in contact until 1979, but no action was taken. The family then moved away. At first, the girls were raped every day, then it settled down to twice or three times a week. He continued to rape them even when there were problems with the pregnancies. No one seemed concerned that the girls became pregnant repeatedly, although there was no other man around.

On occasion, he flung his younger daughter across the room for refusing him sex, resulting in a broken arm. Even this did not ring alarm bells. She told the doctor that she had broken it playing, but her medical records showed she had bruises on her legs and a burn mark on her arm. 'No one was there for us and we were too terrified of him to tell anyone what was happening,' said the elder daughter. 'I pleaded for him to stop but he wouldn't. I was too scared to tell anyone.'

The younger daughter told of the frightening habit her father had of putting her head next to the flames of their gas fire and that when she struggled to get away on certain occasions she burnt her eyes. It left her with permanent scarring.

They were kept out of school when their injuries were

visible and the family moved every six months, living in remote villages in South Yorkshire and Lincolnshire where no one knew them. Rather than employ babysitters, the children were locked in their room when their father went out. There were few visitors and they were kept in isolation. To all intents and purposes, they had disappeared.

He threatened to kill them if they told anyone what they were going through. They believed this because he had a 'one-second fuse'. He also told them that, if they reported him to the police, the social services would take their children away. The sisters grew so desperate that they regularly gave the father a lot of whisky in the hope that he might die. In 1988, suspicions were raised at the victims' school about their injuries, but these were blamed on bullying.

Even when his daughters were grown up he made them stay living under his roof. There would be no escape. The elder daughter became pregnant seven times and had two surviving children. Her younger sister had 12 pregnancies, with 5 surviving children. Two of the sisters' babies died on the day they were born. 'When my mum asked me who the father of my first child was, I told her it was a local boy – but I knew the real father was my dad,' said the elder daughter. 'I lost count of how many times he raped me. As I got older, he said if I told anyone, my children would be taken away from me.'

Their mother claimed that, in the early 1990s, she had contacted social services after arriving at the man's home and hearing him order his daughter, who was getting dressed, to 'come back to bed'. 'I couldn't believe what I was hearing,' she said. 'There was no one else in the house. I rang social services and they took details but said they would need corroboration. I then rang them regularly several times a week for the next six months. I was always being put through to someone different and it never went anywhere.'

A year later, her own mother had reported him to police after catching him in bed with his daughter. 'He stormed in and said to his wife that she had to sort it because her mum had gone to the police,' she said.

The following year, after one of the girls had had a miscarriage, relatives contacted social services again and were shocked by their indifference. Over the phone, they were told, 'We are aware of the family – but do you have an address?'

During their 19 pregnancies, they would have been seen over 100 times by GPs, midwives and other healthcare professionals, but no one investigated their plight. When the younger daughter was pregnant with her first child, the doctor asked whether the baby was her father's – she denied it. But as time went by and the two sisters had multiple miscarriages and terminations, they were advised not to have any more children with the same father. They were also given genetic counselling at one point.

In 1992, the younger daughter collapsed and was rushed to hospital while she was pregnant and she showed her bruises to a health visitor. Both daughters were again seen in hospital when their children were ill.

One daughter would be forced to look after the children while he raped the other. They begged him to stop the torture. The elder daughter once volunteered to give him £100 a month out of her child benefit if he stopped abusing her. Soon, the rape resumed and he took the money anyway.

'At one stage a few years ago, I even paid him a few times from my benefits just to stop him. There was no way out,' the elder daughter said. 'Over the years, I pleaded with him to stop but he didn't. There was no reaction or heart in him. He'd just tell us to go to the bedroom.'

Their brother, who had fled the family at 15, went to Lincolnshire Police in 1997 and told them of his father's incest with his sisters. Again, the allegation was investigated, but no action was taken.

In 1998, the tyrant kicked and punched his younger daughter for meeting up with the son of one of their neighbours. He then attacked his eldest daughter. Holding a knife to her throat, he told her, 'It's never going to end. You have to do what you are told.' Around then, they called ChildLine, but hung up when they got no assurance that they could keep their children. 'We love our kids more than anything in the world,' said the younger daughter. 'Although they were born out of hate, we love them and always will. I don't know how I will be able to tell them who their father is. It is going to be very difficult.'

Even three years after the birth of the last child, he offered his elder daughter £500 to have another child by him.

The family returned to Sheffield in 2004. Lincolnshire social services liaised with those in Sheffield who made numerous visits. It was only four years later that the younger daughter contacted her social worker and reported the abuse. By then, the women had partners of their own; this gave them the courage to come forward. 'It took us years to build up the courage to report him,' said the elder daughter. 'We were just under his control.' It was estimated that the authorities had had over 150 opportunities to stop him, but missed them all.

Their father was arrested in June 2008, only four months after the last rape. It was estimated that he had raped them over a thousand times. During the investigation, Sheffield Police interviewed the girls' mother who denied any wrongdoing and spoke of her husband's domination of family life and his violence. 'We moved away and lost touch,' she said. 'We were aware the girls had had children but not how many, nor who the father was. As soon as we saw the stories on the news, we knew who it would be. My blood ran cold. He is evil but the social services are a disgrace. They should have done something.'

The girls' father denied the charges, but DNA testing confirmed that his daughter's children were his and he was charged with 25 counts of rape. He pleaded guilty and refused to sit in court to face his accusers, although his two daughters appeared in the public gallery for the sentencing. The prosecutor Nicholas Campbell QC outlined the scale of the crimes the defendant had committed. 'All the defendant's children spoke of his domination over their family life. He was tall and strongly built,' he said. 'All the family were frightened of him. When they heard his car pulling up outside the house, the children and their mother ran to their respective rooms. His younger daughter told of the frightening habit her father had of putting her head next to the flames of their gas fire and that when she struggled to get away on certain occasions she burnt her eyes.'

He threatened his daughters with a 'real hiding' if they refused to have sex with him. 'When either one of his victims tried to end the sexual abuse, he threatened to kill them and their children,' said Campbell, 'and when they threatened to tell police, he said they would not be believed. All the time, when the sisters were challenged about the paternity of their children, they would cover it up. They started taking the Pill. He said they should not be taking it and, just as they felt unable to avoid his sexual abuse, they obeyed. They spoke of his pleasure at fathering their children whilst at the same time they had fears for the welfare of these children and how they would cope.'

This was plainly a threat to the women's health. 'The defendant played Russian roulette as to whether there would be complications in the pregnancies and with the health of his daughters,' Campbell said. The court also heard that on a number of occasions doctors advised the women to stop having children by the same father.

Sentencing the prisoner, Judge Alan Goldsack QC said, 'What he did was the grossest possible breach of trust when he should have been protecting his daughters. He has not shown any remorse and has clearly not begun to appreciate the psychological harm he has caused. I can say that in nearly forty years of dealing with criminal cases and fourteen as a family judge, the combination of aggravating circumstances here is the worst I have come across. I have little doubt that many members of the public hearing the facts of this case will consider either you should never be released from prison or only when you are old and infirm. I agree with that view. A criminal justice system which does not reflect the views of the silent majority of the public does not deserve to have its confidence. For centuries, the maximum sentence available for rape has been life imprisonment. That is the sentence I pass, concurrent on each count of rape, with no separate penalty for the indecent assaults.'

The judge also had some harsh words for the rapist's ex-wife. 'Your wife clearly became aware of what was going on but did nothing to assist her daughters. She could have alerted the authorities – but did not.' The defendant was sentenced to 25 simultaneous life sentences and told he must serve a minimum of 19½ years in prison. This was reduced to 14½ years on appeal.

The social services were roundly condemned. 'They should have done something,' said the rapist's cousin. 'Family members were reporting him but it never went anywhere. This could all have been stopped nearly two decades ago.' The cousin who had tried to take action told the *Sun*, 'In 1982, I was worried after discovering he was beating the girls with a belt buckle. I went to the NSPCC in Sheffield but nothing came of it. I felt as though they dismissed it. Then, in 1988, I mentioned to a police sergeant that I believed something horrible was happening and it might be incestuous. The officer was very good and appeared to make enquiries with the social services but they didn't act. I know my uncle's brother also said he'd contacted the authorities.

'Some years later, I spoke to the same police officer. I think he did all he could but social services didn't seem to take any action. The girls' father is just plain evil. On one occasion after his daughter had a miscarriage, he was at our house within hours, wanting to sell us baby stuff because my wife was pregnant. He should now just rot in prison. He should never be released.' He added, 'I believe he was just using his daughters as a way of getting cash out of the system. Every time he got one of them pregnant, he saw it as the chance to claim more benefit. I don't remember him ever working. He obviously loved the control he had over the sisters. He put them through a horrific nightmare lasting nearly three decades.'

Nick Clegg, MP for Sheffield Hallam said, 'I can't imagine a better definition of being evil than torturing your own children in this abusive way. Some of the details are just heart-rending ... All our thoughts are now with the victims of this most abhorrent crime, who must be given the time and privacy to rebuild their lives.'

Prime Minister at the time, Gordon Brown, said, 'The whole country will be outraged by those unspeakable events that have been reported as happening in Sheffield and in other parts of the country and will be utterly appalled by the news of the systemic abuse of two sisters by their father over such a long period. People will want to know how such abuse could go on for so long without the authorities and the wider public services discovering it and taking action. If there is a change to be made in the system and the system has failed, we will change the system.'

The daughters said in a statement, 'His detention in prison brings us only the knowledge that he cannot physically touch us again.' They were given counselling for trauma. 'Now we want to get on with our lives,' they said. 'We don't want anyone to know who we are.'

19

MODERN-DAY SLAVERY

In September 2011, after six weeks of surveillance, 250 officers from the Bedford and Hertfordshire Police raided Greenacres Caravan Park in Little Billington, near Leighton Buzzard. They found 22 men being held in smelly sheds and leaking horse boxes. They were in a shocking state. Many of them were malnourished and suffering from scurvy. They had broken bones and were covered in excrement. Others had scars, flesh wounds and dog bites.

These modern-day slaves were woken at 5.30am each morning and driven across Britain and Europe where they were forced to perform back-breaking manual work up to 19 hours a day laying block-paving driveways. They were used instead of hiring machinery to save money.

Given next to no food, they were paid little or no money. Their overcrowded accommodation had no washing facilities or toilets. They were unable to shower for months at a time, forced to wash in cold water and had to go to the lavatory in a nearby field. Their bedding was washed once every four months and one shed got so cold at night that water froze. One victim compared the conditions to a concentration camp and said he was treated 'worse than a slave'. 'When I looked around at us all, I realized how ill everyone looked – really skinny, dirty and really unwell,' he said. 'It was horrible.'

Yards away, their bosses lived in plush chalets which their victims had to clean. The captives told how they were ordered to forget about their families and should never talk about their past. Instead, they were told to treat the family of travellers holding them captive as their new family. Fifty-two-year-old Tommy Connors Sr was to be called 'Pa' and his wife Mary 'Ma', even though some of the captives were older than they were.

The longest-serving slave had been there for 15 years. The 54-year-old man said he had suffered numerous beatings. He had been hit over the head with a broom handle and punched in the face. A medical examination revealed that, over the years, two of his ribs and his right ankle had been fractured.

In 1996, he had been living on benefits in Brighton when he had met members of the Connors family. They promised him £50 a day in cash and a roof over his head. But over his 15 years in captivity, he had received only £80. He had been taken around Britain and across Europe, working long hours for the travellers' block-paving and scrap-metal businesses. As police took him from the camp, he received a threatening phone call from Tommy Connors Sr.

The oldest slave was 61. During a low point in his life, he

had been spotted at Tamworth service station in a distressed state by James John Connors, who lured him back to the camp with offers of food, drink and tobacco. Instead, he 'suffered seven years of abuse, starvation and torture'. 'There was no respect,' he said. 'They treated me like a slave. And that's putting it mildly.'

The man was an alcoholic. The Connors weaned him off the booze and his life became one long round of 'beatings, starvation and work'. At one point, he slipped and fell through a roof, breaking his ankle. The Connors refused to let him go to hospital; instead, they gave him painkillers to mask the pain. He was kept on hard manual labour for another four weeks before they finally allowed him to seek medical attention.

In October 2010, a 23-year-old man with a muscle-wasting disease was approached as he left the job centre in Southampton. He had fallen on hard times and was sleeping on the streets. They offered him shelter and £60 a day to work for them. As he was being driven towards the travellers' site in Leighton Buzzard, he asked if he could collect his mobile phone so he could contact his mother. 'You don't need it,' he was told. 'Your mother is dead to you now. Your family is dead to you now.' Later, when he tried to tell them about the pain his disease was causing him, they told him, 'Travellers don't feel pain.' After five months, the Connors let him go because he had been reported as a missing person.

The police were finally alerted to the camp when a 38-year-old man escaped. While out canvassing for the family's block-paving business, he seized the opportunity to flag down a police car. He told the police that he had been forced to carry out tough manual work for 16 hours a day and described how he was regularly assaulted, mentally tortured and treated worse than a slave. He was forced to hand over his benefits and had been threatened with death if he tried to escape. 'I didn't like it,' he told the police. 'But they said I couldn't leave and said if I tried to leave ... I would get murdered.'

On one occasion, he was punched in the eye by a member of the Connors family for failing to drum up enough business. 'He pulled up in the car and said, "What have you been doing? Why haven't you got any customers? Aren't you ashamed of yourself?"' the victim said. 'Then he shoved me in the boot of his car. He said, "Get in there." I went in head first. He quickly slammed down the boot.' While in the boot of the car he was forced to sing the children's songs 'How Much is that Doggy in the Window?' and 'Bob the Builder'.

Among the men being held were a former priest and a Gulf War veteran. Their heads were shaved and they were given uniforms to mark them out as slaves. Though there were 22 slaves on the site when the police raided it, many more had passed through over the years. Detectives believe hundreds of vulnerable men had been picked up at soup kitchens, night shelters and job centres by the Connors who offered them work over the preceding 30 years. They made millions of pounds by forcing the men to work for no pay. The Connors themselves insisted on being paid in cash. It was estimated that one man alone was owed £70,000.

After the raid on the camp, the focus of the investigation widened when police forces in Eastern European countries and Russia said they had discovered that local criminals had links to the Connors. Arrests were made under legislation passed in 2010 that made slavery, servitude and forced labour a criminal offence. The case was described in court as the first 'quasi-slavery trial in this country for over two hundred years'.

In July 2012, husband and wife team – James John, 34, and Josie Connors, 31, who are also cousins – were jailed for 11 and 4 years respectively at Luton Crown Court. Judge Michael Kay QC said, 'The way they brutally manipulated and exploited men is pure evil. It is at odds with the moral code of the religion they profess to hold. Their disdain for the dignity of others is shocking. They were not Good Samaritans but violent, cold, hard exploiters.'

Mother of three, Josie Connors, had 'reacted badly' to being remanded in custody, the court was told. 'She is not very well,' Karen Walton said for the defence. 'She has been on watch in the prison service. For a traveller to be static has a much more detrimental effect than on other people in our society.'

James John Connor, also known as 'Big Jim', was also convicted of assault occasioning actual bodily harm. Josie's father Tommy Connors Sr and her brother Patrick were also convicted. Other members of the family also faced charges. The complainants could not be named for legal reasons.

In court, prosecutor Frances Oldham QC said, 'Physical violence and the threat of such violence, whether spoken or unspoken, was regularly used to ensure compliance with demands for work, to stop any attempt to claim the promised wages and to instil a fear of retribution if any worker attempted to escape the clutches of the Connors family.'

Talking of the elderly man taken from Tamworth service station in 2004, the judge said, 'He was an alcoholic. In three months, he was weaned off alcohol. Your purpose was to put him to work. After he had been rescued by police, he was reluctant to speak about what had happened, his mind having been manipulated. Even though he was considerably older than both of you, he believed you were his surrogate parents. After he had overcome the trauma, he spoke more openly. He lived in a caravan with no toilets or washing facilities, he had to go to the toilet in a nearby field. Sometimes, the only food available was eggs and bread.'

The man had to work from 5.00am to around 9.00pm on driveways and then had to clean the Connors' caravan to 'an immaculate standard'. 'He said he was beaten and practically starved, he was punched, kicked and hit with a broom handle,' the judge said.

According to the judge, the man who had escaped and alerted the police had been recruited in Wembley and was offered £80 a day for work. 'He received no pay, his personal possessions and documents were taken away,' Judge Kay said. 'Conditions were squalid and, at times, they were starving. Josie said if he used the toilets in their caravan, she would break his arms and legs. He said he was being mentally tortured and felt worse than a slave.' He described being 'kicked in the nuts' on one occasion and, on another day, being punched in the eye for not finding any work.

The judge insisted that the trial was not racist and did not seek to single out the Irish traveller community. 'This is not about racism or the way of life of Irish travellers,' he said. 'It is about a capacity to be inhumane to a fellow human being.'

20

THE BELGIAN BASEMENT

Ariel Castro showed a preference for young girls; Michelle Knight was 21 when he kidnapped her, Amanda Berry was 16, Gina DeJesus 14 and it was feared that he would have gone on to kidnap girls who were younger and younger. In the 1990s, in Belgium, paedophile Marc Dutroux set about doing the same thing, but only two of his six sex slaves survived.

One of the survivors was Belgian schoolgirl Sabine Dardenne. She was 12 years old when she was kidnapped cycling to school in Tournai, 50 miles (85km) south-west of Brussels in the French-speaking half of the country. Often, she met her friend Davina along the way. But on 28 May 1996, there was no sign of Davina, so she continued alone. As she was cycling along the high wall of the local football stadium, she heard the sound of a vehicle coming up behind her. A rusty old camper van pulled up beside her. The side door slid open and a man leaned out. He plucked her from her bike and threw her in the back. It was all over in less than a second.

Sabine was small for her age and there was no way she could fight off her abductor, who was a fully grown man. He shoved pills in her mouth and tied her up in a blanket. The van pulled to a halt. Her abductor collected her bike and the school bag she had dropped and threw them into the van, leaving no clue as to her disappearance.

Although she was beginning to feel drowsy, she was scared and began to cry. She could not see where they were going but, from the sound of the wheels, she guessed they were heading on to the motorway. Pretending to be asleep, she tried to overhear what her kidnappers were saying. They were Flemish speakers from the north. But it was clear from their conversation that the man in the back of the van who had grabbed her was in charge. The driver was just 'a loser', she said later. When the van stopped, she was bent double and forced into a trunk. When it was opened again, she found herself in a room with the man who had grabbed her. He had a moustache, greasy hair and horrible eyes, she said.

The blinds were drawn and the room was a mess. There was a cot and some toys in the corner and, on top of the fridge, a telephone. It was too high up for her to reach. Next to it there was a staircase and a door with planks nailed across it. She never found out what went on in the room beyond. Her abductor took her upstairs and told her to undress. Once she was naked, he put a chain around her neck and left her there overnight.

The next day, he told her that he had saved her life. His boss had wanted to kill her for revenge. Sabine's father had been in the police force. Instead, he had persuaded his boss to ransom her parents. He was now asking her parents for 3 million francs for her return. Sabine figured that her parents might be able to raise 1 million, but 3 million was out of the question. If they did not get the money, it was clear that they intended to kill her.

The two men took Polaroid pictures of her naked in her chains. Then the man with the moustache took her to another bedroom and sexually abused her on the double bed. He thought she should have enjoyed this and her crying annoyed him.

Later, she complained about being kept naked all the time and she was given some clothes when they went downstairs to eat. But she was regularly taken upstairs for more photographic sessions and more sexual abuse.

She was told that her parents had refused to pay the ransom and she was in grave danger as his boss wanted to kill her again. Her abductor now cast himself in the role of her saviour. He would hide her somewhere safe.

Downstairs, hidden behind some shelving there was a large concrete door. Behind it were stairs that led down to a junk-filled cellar. It was lit by two lightbulbs. It was so dirty and dank that Sabine feared she might suffocate down there, until he showed her the ventilation system made out of the fan from an old computer. The cellar was just 3ft wide and 9ft long (1m by 3m). Along one side was a metal cage containing a bed made from wooden slats with a filthy mattress that was falling apart. At the bottom of the bed there was just enough room to put a chamber pot and Sabine's school satchel. To one side, there was a table and a bench. On the other was a plank that served as a shelf she put her glasses and crayons on. High up on another shelf was an old TV set connected to a Sega games console. The walls had been freshly painted bright yellow. Had this hell-hole been decorated just for her?

He brought her some bread, milk and jerry cans full of water. These were emergency provisions, he said, in case he could not come to feed her for any reason. Her situation was horrible, but Sabine comforted herself with the idea that the whole of Belgium was looking for her by then. Meanwhile, she had her French homework to do.

Indeed, police helicopters were searching the area from which she had disappeared. Her picture and description appeared on walls across the country. As hope faded, Sabine Dardenne joined a list of other missing girls. This included 8-year-old Julie Lejeune and Melissa Russo who had disappeared in June 1995, and 17-year-old An Marchal and 19-year-old Eefje Lambrecks who had gone missing together two months later. Two months after Sabine had disappeared, another name would be added to the list. It belonged to 14½-year-old Laetitia Delhez, who disappeared on 9 August 1996.

Sabine's abductor was Marc Dutroux. A dangerous paedophile, he was born in Ixelles, Belgium, in 1956, the oldest of five children. His parents separated in 1971 and Dutroux stayed with his mother. He married at 19 and fathered 2 children, then divorced in 1983. By then, he had taken up with Michelle Martin who shared his interest. In 1986, they were arrested for the abduction and rape of five young girls. Martin got 5 years, Dutroux 13. In prison, they married. They were both released early for good behaviour and went on to have three children together.

By the mid-1990s Dutroux was living on welfare. To supplement his income, he went into the sex trade. By 1996, he owned seven houses in Belgium. Most of them stood vacant and were the perfect venues to use for filming the girls he kidnapped for use in pornographic videos, then to sell on as prostitutes.

The police knew all about this. In 1993, an informant reported that Dutroux had offered him over 100,000 Belgian francs (£2,000) to kidnap young girls. Two years later, the same informant told the police that Dutroux was building a dungeon in which to incarcerate girls. Indeed, Dutroux's own mother informed prosecutors that her son had been keeping young girls in empty houses, but no one followed up.

In the cellar, Dutroux worked on Sabine psychologically. It was not that her parents would not pay the ransom – they simply didn't care enough about her. As far as they were concerned, she was dead and they had already packed away all her things. The police had given up looking for her and, if his boss found her, he would kill her. If she wanted to live, Dutroux said, there was only one person she could depend on – and that was him.

To stay alive, she was to remain perfectly quiet. His boss was often in the house; if he heard her cry out, he would come and kill her. She should occupy herself quietly with her schoolbooks and the Sega game. When it was safe, he would come and take her upstairs to get something to eat or do 'other things'. When he did, he would come to the door and say, 'It's me,' before opening it. If anyone else came, she should keep absolutely quiet and lie perfectly still. Dutroux also described in terrifying detail how his boss would torture her before he killed her. She also thought that she must do everything she could to please Dutroux. Otherwise, he would grow tired of her and dispose of her himself. He had a gun; he showed it to her.

Her life became a cycle of hell. When she was not in her filthy cage in the cellar, she would be upstairs eating something Dutroux had prepared, which was generally inedible. Afterwards, she would be taken to the bedroom where she would have to do whatever he wanted, no matter how disgusting she found it, while watching fuzzy pornographic films on a satellite channel. Then it was back to the cellar.

Even ordinary daily activities became almost unendurable. When she wanted a wash, he would wash her himself, which meant having a bath together. During this hideous ordeal, he would scrub her so hard that she would end up covered in red sores.

Sabine kept an eye out for ways to escape, but Dutroux always kept between her and the front door. Even if she got outside, she did not know where she was and could not have got far before he grabbed her.

Sabine fought back; she would ask when she could go home and see her parents, and pester him for better food, a pillow for her bed, clean clothes, paper to draw on, even a toothbrush. She refused to drink curdled milk or eat mouldy bread. But, in the end, she had to take what she was given and was forced to eat rancid mincemeat while he feasted on steak.

Could she at least use the phone to call her parents? He said that the line had to be kept open in case they called to agree to the ransom demand. But hadn't they refused to pay? He then said that the phone on top of the fridge was the hot line to the boss. If she tried to use it, she would get through to the boss and she knew what the result would be. The boss was richer and more powerful than the prime minister, he said.

Eventually, she badgered him into buying her a clock-radio. She could, at least, listen to music, although he had somehow barred the news channels. The numbers on the clock comforted her. Each was tied to something in her former life – her father's age, her mother's birthday, the number of her grandmother's house. She also demanded a new mattress; the one she had was falling apart and there were insects inside it. Sabine had a horror of insects and her body was covered with bites. Eventually, he came and sprayed it with insecticide.

As well as keeping up with her schoolwork, she used an exercise book to record the terrible things he did to her. He also allowed her to write a letter to her mother which, he said, a friend would deliver. Her mother's response, he said, was that she should eat properly, wash and enjoy the sex. According to Dutroux, she also said that, as they could not afford to pay the ransom, she should make the best of it and accept her position as Dutroux's girlfriend. Sabine did not really believe that her mother had said these things, but she could not be absolutely sure the letter had not been delivered.

On 21 June, Dutroux announced that he was being sent on a 'mission'. While this meant that Sabine would be spared doing 'other things', it also meant that she would have to stay locked in the cellar and she was afraid of the dark. She could not stand the dark, so he left the light on all the time. He left her with extra provisions – tinned tomatoes and meatballs, mouldy bread and biscuits – but she also had to face the prospect that he would not return and she would be left there for ever.

But Dutroux did return – and things got worse. Instead of being left in the cellar at night, he forced her to sleep next to him, chaining her to the bed. But she could not sleep in case he started doing things. To maintain her self-esteem, she had to put up at least token resistance. Her strategy was to drive him mad with her whining. She complained about everything she would think of – not being able to telephone her parents, her chain not being long enough, not having a *TV Guide*. At other times she would call him an 'arsehole' or a 'shit', or tell him that he was not normal because of the things he was doing to her. It made no difference; he seemed to enjoy her distress, so eventually she kept quiet. From a sideways glance at the post, she discovered his name and address. She was in Marcinelle, a suburb of Charteroi, some 50 miles (80km) from her home in Tournai.

While she hated having him around, things were worse when he went away. She found the cellar claustrophobic; it was either too cold or too hot. She could not wash or clean her teeth down there, or even empty her chamber pot. He was away for as much as six days at a time and she could not get away from the stench.

On one occasion, the power went off and the ventilation fan stopped. Although she had been told to keep quiet, she was afraid that she was going to suffocate and started screaming. No one came and, after a while, the electricity came back on again. However, screaming had emboldened her. She braced herself against the wall. Pushing with all her might, she managed to move the concrete door just an inch. But then it jammed. Dutroux was furious when he returned. He said that his boss might have seen it and killed her. She never tried to open it again.

As well as being his slave in the bedroom, Dutroux extended her duties to the rest of the house. She had to make his coffee, although she was not allowed any herself. And she had to clean the house, although not the cellar. With no washing machine, her clothes grew filthy. Occasionally, she got the chance to wash out her panties in the bathroom.

She wrote more letters about the terrible things she underwent at Dutroux's hands. They were never sent. One was found under Dutroux's mattress. Thankfully, it was unopened. After she was released, Sabine did not want her mother to know what she had endured and Dutroux had not enjoyed any perverted pleasure from reading it. Nevertheless, it became an important piece of evidence and was read by the jury when Dutroux finally faced trial.

After months of the sexual abuse, Dutroux finally raped Sabine. He showed no sympathy for the physical suffering he put her through, let alone the mental anguish. She was left in terrible pain and haemorrhaged badly, and she was afraid that she was going to die from loss of blood alone in her underground prison. Why didn't he put her out of her misery with a bullet in the head?

She put all her hope in her letters. Fearing that, in some way, she was being punished, she begged her parents to allow her to come home. But she knew in her heart of hearts that they were not being delivered, so she devised a simple test. She wrote a letter in the form of a questionnaire; it was returned filled in. Clearly, the handwriting was not her mother's. Nor were the simple grammatical mistakes.

As her captivity dragged on, Sabine finished reading all her books and was fed up with the Sega game station. The only person to talk to was Dutroux, whose stock reply was, 'Shut up.' It was summer and she pestered him to go out in the sunshine. In response, he shoved two chairs together and forced her to sunbathe – naked – in the front room.

She also badgered him about seeing her friends – with unforeseen consequences. He brought her one. One day, after a 'sunbathing' session, she was taken upstairs where she found another girl naked and chained to the bed. She asked Sabine how long she had been there and was not pleased to hear the answer was 77 days.

The new girl was 14-year-old Laetitia Delhez; she had been snatched in Bertrix on the French border. She had been walking home when an old van pulled up alongside her and Dutroux leant out and grabbed her. Laetitia soon joined Sabine down in the cellar and brought important news. She had seen Sabine's picture on posters. Neither her parents nor the police had given up looking for her. With the two of them in the cellar, the air became more fetid than ever. It was a relief when Dutroux came to take Laetitia upstairs, although Sabine knew what was going to happen to her.

After the first time Laetitia was raped, Dutroux stopped coming. A couple of days passed and Sabine figured that he must be on a 'mission'. In fact, on 13 August 1996, Dutroux, his wife Michelle Martin and the driver Michel Lelièvre had been arrested.

The abduction of Laetitia Delhez had not gone as smoothly as that of Sabine. There was an eyewitness who had managed to note down part of the licence plate number. This matched the one on a van registered to known sex offender Marc Dutroux. An officer from the child protection squad was sent to the house, but found nothing. Later, he was castigated for this, but Sabine said that he could hardly be blamed as the entrance to the dungeon was masterfully concealed.

Two days later, Laetitia and Sabine heard a noise upstairs. The shelves were being cleared and they could hear bricks being chiselled from the walls. The two girls were terrified. Fearing the boss was coming to kill them, they hid under the blanket.

There were footstep and men's voices. Then Dutroux's voice said, 'It's me.' Still fearing the worst, Sabine lay still. But Laetitia recognized one of the other men – he was a policeman she knew from Bertrix. Sabine was still hesitant and turned to Dutroux to ask if she could leave. He said she could – and she could take her crayons with her.

As Sabine and Laetitia left the cellar, both gave Dutroux a kiss on the cheek.

Once above ground, Sabine flung herself on to the nearest policeman and would not let him go, while Laetitia clung on to the policeman from Bertrix. Then, after 80 days, Sabine was taken out into the sunshine and fresh air. It was only at the station that Sabine discovered the police had given up any hope of finding her alive long ago. It was Laetitia they were looking for when they visited Dutroux's house.

When Sabine arrived back in Tournai, she learned that thousands of people had been out looking for her. The search had been co-ordinated by the missing-persons' centre set up earlier to look for Julie Lejeune and Melissa Russo, then An Marchal and Eefje Lambrecks.

Two days after Sabine and Laetitia's release, the bodies of Julie Lejeune and Melissa Russo were found buried in the garden of a house Dutroux owned in Sars-la-Buissière. After being raped repeatedly, the two girls had starved to death in captivity when Dutroux had been imprisoned for car theft in December 1995. Sabine and Laetitia had been at risk of suffering the same fate.

Dutroux denied responsibility for the deaths of Julie and Melissa, saying that he had told his accomplice Bernard Weinstein to feed them. When he discovered that Weinstein had not followed his instructions, he drugged the man with barbiturates and buried him alive. His body was found alongside Julie and Melissa's in Sars-la-Buissière.

While being interviewed by the police, Sabine discovered that she had only been rescued because, after his arrest, the driver Michel Lelièvre had admitted to having been involved in the kidnapping of Laetitia. When the police then told Dutroux that the game was up, he admitted that he was holding two girls. At the time, the police were only looking for Laetitia. Dutroux then led the police to them.

In Dutroux's house, the police found over 300 porno-graphic videos featuring children; 6,000 hair samples taken from the dungeon were analysed to see if other victims had been kept there. Meanwhile, Lelièvre admitted to kid-napping An Marchal and Eefje Lambrecks while they were on a camping trip to the Belgian port of Ostend. Then there had been four captives at the house in Marcinelle – Julie and Melissa in the dungeon, with An and Eefje chained up upstairs. Eefje had made several escape attempts. In one, she managed to get out on to the roof, but Dutroux caught her. Eventually, the two older girls were so troublesome, he drugged them and buried them alive. Their bodies were found under a shed next to another house owned by Dutroux and occupied by Weinstein.

The arrest of Dutroux spawned a larger scandal. He was part of a paedophile ring involving leading members of Belgian society. Nine police officers in Charleroi were detained for questioning over possible negligence. A parliamentary committee investigating the matter said that failures in the investigation led to the deaths of four girls who could have been saved. Meanwhile, 300,000 protestors took to the streets of Brussels in the largest demonstration in Belgium since the Second World War.

The police then made another gaffe. When Dutroux was allowed to travel to Neufchâteau to consult files he would use in his forthcoming trial, he attacked his guards, grabbed a gun, stole a car and made a break for it. As helicopters circled above, Sabine was given an armed guard. Dutroux soon gave himself up, but his escape forced the resignation of the state police chief, the minister of justice and the minister of the interior.

Dutroux's escape brought charges for assault and theft. He was sentenced to five years. But his trial for kidnapping, rape and murder was delayed when a magazine in Luxembourg printed the names of 50 alleged paedophiles said to have come from the Dutroux investigation. Dutroux stalled things further by claiming that the Belgian state was violating his human rights by keeping him in solitary confinement and performing frequent body searches. The

Belgian people were outraged at this, considering what he had put his victims through.

Then an unauthorized interview was aired on Belgian TV. In it, Dutroux was heard to admit keeping Julie, Melissa, An and Eefje, effectively admitting his guilt. Then a hearing had to be convened to establish the authenticity and admissibility of this evidence. So his trial for the substantive charges of murder, rape and kidnapping was postponed repeatedly. It was over seven years before the case came to court.

The trial eventually began on 1 March 2004. At it, Dutroux maintained that he was merely a pawn in the paedophile ring masterminded by Jean-Michel Nihoul. Dutroux also claimed that two police officers helped in the kidnapping of An Marchal and Eefje Lambrecks. Then a key to his handcuffs was found in his cell, apparently smuggled in in a bag of salt.

The showdown came on 19 April 2004, when Sabine Dardenne, now aged 20, took the stand. She rejected out of hand the apology he gave in court. Meeting his stare across the courtroom, she forced him to lower his eyes. After Laetitia Delhez testified, the jury were taken to view the dungeon where they had been held. When they returned, Dutroux admitted the kidnapping and rape, but he denied murder, blaming Martin, Lelièvre and Nihoul.

In the end, Dutroux was found guilty of kidnapping and raping all six girls, and murdering An Marchel, Eefje Lambrecks and Bernard Weinstein. Lelièvre was found guilty of kidnapping, but acquitted of murder. Martin was convicted of kidnapping and rape. The jury could not agree a verdict in Nihoul's case. Eventually, he was acquitted of involvement in the abduction of the girls, but was convicted of human trafficking and drugs charges.

Dutroux was sentenced to life and put at 'the government's disposition'. That meant, if he was ever paroled, the government could return him to prison. Lelièvre received 25 years; Martin 30; Nihoul five.

Sabine Dardenne continued to feel guilt over Laetitia's incarceration, whom she believes was abducted because she asked for a friend. But Laetitia did not blame her. Indeed, if Laetitia had not been kidnapped, Sabine would probably have died in captivity like the other girls and Dutroux would have remained free to abduct and abuse others.

21

GIRL IN
THE CELLAR

When Elisabeth Fritzl emerged from the cellar in 2008, everyone was reminded of another Austrian girl who had emerged from a cellar just two years earlier. Her name was Natascha Kampusch and she was just ten years old when she disappeared on 2 March 1998.

Natascha's parents had broken up soon after she was born. She was raised by her mother, but had not lost touch with her father. She had a stable childhood, although she was a persistent bed-wetter. However, throughout her childhood there was a general atmosphere of disquiet. 'Hardly a month went by during my primary school years that the media didn't report yet another abducted, raped or murdered girl,' she said.

In her book *3,096 Days*, she listed 13 incidents of young girls being molested or killed that were reported on the news during those years. Parents and teachers warned about the dangers. At school, pupils were shown films where girls were molested by their older brothers, or boys learned to defy an abusive father. The message was hammered home – never accept sweets from a stranger, never get into a car with a stranger. She even recalled a psychologist advising victims not to resist their attackers as they risked being killed. Natascha comforted herself that she was not the skinny blonde that child molesters seemed to prefer.

Shortly before she disappeared, she had spent the weekend with her father. When he brought her home, he let her walk across the dark courtyard of the apartment block where her mother lived on her own – only to find that her mother was not at home. Sensibly, she sought refuge in the apartment of a neighbour. But when her mother turned up, she was furious. Natascha, she said, was never to see her father again.

Natascha was fed up with rows between her parents; she looked forward to turning 18, so she could move out. Determined to become self-reliant, she persuaded her mother to allow her to walk to school on her own. But in the street, she got cold feet. Despite her tears, she continued on her way.

In a quiet back street, a slim young man was standing by a white delivery van. His eyes were strangely vacant, she noticed. The rapes and murders she had seen on TV came to mind. Then her worst nightmare began; he grabbed her and threw her into the van.

Her memory of the event was hazy. She could remember one of those silent screams you have in dreams where you open your mouth and nothing comes out. She had no memory of fighting back, but the following day she had a black eye and must have been stunned by a blow. All the time, she was thinking that this could not really be happening to her.

Her abductor was 36-year-old Wolfgang Priklopil, a communications technician who still lived with his mother. He told her to sit down on the floor in the back of the van and not move. Initially, Natascha thought she was being kidnapped for ransom, but neither of her parents had any money.

She thought that it would be a good idea to talk to her captor, and used the familiar '*du*' form of address one uses with family and friends. The first thing she asked him was his shoe size. *Aktenzeichen XY ... ungelöst* – 'File Reference XI ... Unsolve', the German-language equivalent of the UK's *Crimewatch* – stressed the importance of the exact description of the criminal. Priklopil told her to keep quiet.

Convinced that she was going to die, Natascha asked him whether he was going to molest her. He said she was too young for him, but he was going to hand her over to other men who might want her. She had fallen into the hands of one of those paedophile rings she had heard of.

Priklopil tried to make calls from his mobile phone, but got no reply. He drove out to a pine forest outside Vienna, where he stopped. The men he expected to meet were not there. They headed back towards the Gänserndorf where Natascha's grandmother lived and on to Strasshof, a small town nearby. Stopping in a garage of a private house, Priklopil wrapped her in a blanket and carried her indoors. He took her down into the basement where there was a pallet bed, a stainless steel sink and a toilet without a lid. The walls were covered with oak panelling like a sauna. In fact, this small dungeon had been built, like Fritzl's, as an air-raid shelter during the Cold War.

Natasha begged him to let her go. She would say nothing; if he did not keep her overnight, he would not get into trouble. But her words fell on deaf ears. There was nothing she could do except accept the situation and make herself at home.

He left, locking the door. She consoled herself with the thought that her parents would miss her and be better to her in future, and her schoolfriends would think she was a hero. He returned later with a mattress, a toothbrush, toothpaste, a hair brush and other things she had asked him for, along with some of her favourite chocolate biscuits. Then, curiously, he searched her school bag in case she had a radio transmitter hidden in there. Already, she felt that the small room was closing in on her and asked him to read a bedtime story and give her a kiss goodnight. But when he left, the illusion of normality was shattered.

In the morning, she bombarded him with questions. Why was she there? What was going to happen to her? How long was he going to keep her? The police were looking for her, she said. They would find her and he would go to jail. All he said was that he would let her go soon.

Alone again, she made a detailed study of her cell. It was lit by a single bulb that was on 24 hours a day. When it was unscrewed, not a single chink of light entered the room from outside. Nor was there any sound except that of the ventilation fan that whirred 24 hours a day. It was six paces long and four paces wide – 8ft 10in by 7ft 10in (2.7m by 2.4m). It was also about 7ft 10in (2.4m) high and contained some 400cu ft (11,327 litres) of musty air. She tried hammering on the wall; no one came. Soon, she gave way to total despair.

Natascha's absence was noted at school, but it was only when she did not come home that evening that her mother called the police. They searched the area with helicopters and dogs, but no clue was found and the search was called off after three days. When posters of the missing girl went up, reports of sightings flooded in. A 12-year-old girl said she had seen Natascha being pulled into a white van, but at first the police did not take this seriously.

For some time, Natascha continued to believe that, at any moment, the police might burst in and rescue her. But gradually this hope faded and she began to realize that Priklopil had been planning her imprisonment for some time. She was right. While the cell itself had been built by Priklopil's father and grandfather years before, he had recently sought advice on soundproofing from his colleague Ernst Holzapfel.

Natascha found Priklopil's behaviour puzzling. Sometimes, she felt her presence was a burden; at other times, he seemed quite caring, checking she had cleaned her teeth properly and cutting her fingernails. He refused her chewing gum in case she choked on it and he peeled oranges for her, feeding them to her segment by segment. But Natascha complained that he was treating her like a small child. On the other hand, he bought her the food she asked for. Later, he brought her a hot plate and a small electric oven, along with tinned food, so she could cook for herself.

Natascha knew that, at the end of the Second World War, Austrian women stuck thin slices of lemon peel to their skin to make it look like they had some terrible disease to avoid being raped by Russian soldiers. She did this and begged Priklopil to take her to the doctor. He was not taken in and, as a punishment, he turned the light off, leaving her in total darkness.

The loneliness of being in the cellar was unbearable, so she got him to play games with her. He then brought her a computer – a Commodore 64 – with games on it to keep her occupied while he was away. Any comfort she drew from this was undermined by his hints that other men might come and photograph her and do 'other things' to her. It was difficult to sleep at night.

It was cold in the cellar, so he gave her sweaters left over from his military career and he brought her an electric fire. He also brought her a sun-lounger and returned her school things to her, although he burnt her school bag and the shoes that her mother had given her for her birthday.

Putting aside her own fears, Natascha worried about what her mother was going through. She tried to get him to send a letter, saying that she was still alive. It was filled with clues as to where she might be. He refused to send it, but when she persisted, he appeared to give in. The next day, he appeared with an injured finger. The people who had ordered her kidnapping would not allow him to send it and had grabbed the letter out of his hand.

Nevertheless, he let her record a message, which he promised to play down the phone to her mother on her birthday. But he changed his mind. Like Dutroux, he told his captive that her parents would not pay the ransom because they did not love her and did not want her back.

Natascha was smart enough not believe that and, on her first Mother's Day in captivity, she made her mother a card using paper and crayons. She also began collecting information about her kidnapper. She asked him his age; he also told her his name, then thought better of it and gave the name of a friend instead. Once he said that he had picked her out from a school picture. Usually, he said that she was a stray cat he was taking care of. Only later did he say that she was his slave.

Looking back, Natascha Kampusch said she was still young enough to adapt herself to the ways of adults. If she had been any older, she would not have been able to do this. It saved her life.

Priklopil brought a table and chairs down into the cellar and they would eat together. For Natascha, this was preferable to hours of loneliness. He would bring warm water down so she could bathe. But she would have to undress in front of him, then he would wash her down. She was old enough to be abashed at being naked in front of him, but she said he was neither salacious nor particularly tender. He washed in a way that someone might wash a car or a household appliance.

After a month, in the absence of any other lead, the police began to follow up on the report of the 12-year-old girl who had seen Natascha being bundled into a white van and began checking up on the 700 owners of white vans in that part of Austria. When they came to see Priklopil, he said that he had been at home on the day that Natascha had disappeared. Naturally, he had no witness to this. Even so, the police accepted his story and they left without even looking at the vehicle. Priklopil was so sure that they would not be able find his secret dungeon that he invited them to look round. They declined and left.

Two days later, an anonymous caller said that a white van of the type the police were looking for was parked outside Heinestrasse 60 in Strasshof – Priklopil's home. The owner, the caller said, was a 'loner' who lived there with his elderly mother and was thought to have a sexual penchant for children. They also gave a good description of Priklopil.

Another witness called from Vienna. On the morning Natascha had disappeared, they had seen a white van with Gänserndorf licence plates in the vicinity. Strasshof was in the Gänserndorf administrative district. Still the police took no action.

Natascha had already given up hope. As her parents would not pay the ransom, Priklopil said, she would have to stay with him for ever. He could not let her go because she had seen his face. In her dungeon, Natascha was reading *Alice's Adventures in Wonderland*. She, too, was trapped in an underground world that did not make any sense. She asked him for a calendar and clock, so she could keep track of the date and time. She wanted a clock with a loud tick, which she thought would be a comfort. She also asked for cleaning products, so she could keep the cellar spic and span. They should be scented with lavender, so she could imagine she was outdoors. And she began drawing. That way, she could have an interior life, rather than be merely a plaything of Priklopil's.

He brought her a television set with a video player and cassettes of programmes he had recorded. From the news, he edited out reports about her disappearance as he wanted her to believe that neither her parents nor anyone else was looking for her. Later, he brought her a radio. He fixed it so that it only received Czech stations, so she could listen to music but she couldn't understand what anyone was saying. After two years, he reckoned that the search for her was over. Then he gave her a regular radio, so she could listen to Austrian stations.

He also bought her a Walkman, but restricted her supplies of books and tapes for minor infractions, such as using too much air freshener or singing. Otherwise, he would restrict his visits. Normally, he would come once in the morning and again in the evening. But he sometimes delivered an armful of ready meals on Thursday, then disappeared until Sunday evening. He put the lights on a timer. But Natascha had to live with the fact that, if there was a fire, or a burst pipe, or if she choked on a fish bone or something happened to him, she would die down there alone.

Eventually, she badgered him into installing a primitive intercom. If she needed something, she would press a button and a light would go on upstairs. This did not necessarily bring him running, especially at weekends when – she found out later – his mother visited. Later, he added a speaker system, which he used to control her life. He would tell her when to brush her teeth, turn the TV off, read her book, do her maths assignment, eat her food. But Natascha found a way to disable this. Once he twigged that she was not listening, the security was so tight, it would take him up to an hour to open all the doors to get to her. For that period, she had a little peace.

However, he replaced the first intercom with a new two-way system that she could not turn off. This allowed him to eavesdrop on her 24 hours a day. If he was convinced that she was not doing exactly what he told her, he could turn the volume up painfully loud. Otherwise, he would come and take away her prized possessions. She even feared that he might install hidden cameras, so she filled every crack in the wood panelling with toothpaste.

As time passed, he became more of a martinet – she was not to look him in the face, not to speak unless spoken to and do everything she was told to the letter. Even her demeanour was to be totally submissive and she was to call him 'Master'. She refused and, eventually, he dropped the matter. He also told her that she was to be grateful that he had 'saved her'. She could not comply with this either. However, she was grateful that he had neither raped nor killed her.

Although he aimed to have absolute power over her, she realized that he was, in fact, a weak man and, when something went wrong, she said she forgave him. Appearing contrite, he said he would give her anything she wanted, except her freedom. Aware that he had problems with physical intimacy, she wanted a hug. It took her some time to train him to hold her not too loosely and not too tight.

After six months' captivity, Natascha grew depressed because her classmates would be moving up a grade and she would be left behind. To lighten her mood, she asked him if she could have a scented bath like the ones her mother used to prepare for her. Eventually, he gave in. It would have to take place upstairs. There would be no opportunity to escape, he said. All the doors and windows were booby-trapped with explosives. If she opened one, she would blow herself up. And if she screamed, he would have to kill her.

On her journey to the bathroom, she finally saw how

securely she was held. Beyond the stout wood door of her cell, there was a heavy concrete door made out of concrete. Later, she discovered that it was hermitically sealed, so if the ventilation system had failed, she would have suffocated. Beyond the door was a low-ceilinged, narrow passageway, only 27in (68cm) high and 19in (14cm) wide. Crawling through this, they emerged in a maintenance pit in the garage. The entrance was hidden behind a dresser and a safe. The pit itself was covered with floorboards with a trap door cut in them. Natascha realized that, even if the police had searched the house, they would never have found the cell.

As they ascended the stairs to the bathroom, Priklopil reminded her of the consequences of escape. He ran her a bubble bath and, despite her protests, stayed while she undressed. After she had a long soak, he towelled her dry and took her back to her dungeon.

That autumn, Priklopil decided to paint her cell. Natascha was allowed to pick the colour. The fumes made her nauseous. He also brought bookcases, cupboards and a bunk bed. But while assembling them, he grew angry and threw a drill at her. Fortunately, she saw it coming, ducked, and it missed. All the new furniture took up space and her cell became even more claustrophobic.

At Christmas, the floor space was reduced even further by a plastic tree. He was generous with presents. She got everything she asked for, including a small educational computer, a pad of drawing paper and paints. But she confined herself to watercolours as the turpentine needed for the oil paints would emit harmful fumes in a confined space. She took pleasure in painting pictures of her parents, which she hid from Priklopil.

THE DISAPPEARED

On her first New Year's Eve in the dungeon, she was left there alone in complete darkness as Priklopil saw the New Year in with his only friend Ernst Holzapfel. They set off fireworks. In later years, she was allowed upstairs to watch them and, when she was 16, she was allowed out into the garden. After the New Year, she was allowed upstairs to take a shower once every two weeks. Sometimes, he would let her stay upstairs to eat and watch TV. Every moment spent outside the cell was precious, but spending time around her captor had another effect. Constantly hamstrung by his petty rules, her power to resist began to diminish. After she had returned to the cellar, he meticulously wiped anything she had touched to get rid of the fingerprints and he was convinced that, sooner or later, the police would return.

He bought her a Horse-Riding Barbie Doll and encouraged her to make new outfits for her. Secretly, she made presents for her family. Though there was little chance she would ever be able to give them to them, it boosted her morale. If she even mentioned her parents, he flew into a rage. He was her family now, he said – she belonged to him. When this made her cry, he would lock her back in her cell and turn off the lights until she was 'good' again.

Priklopil was creating his own private world where he was the most important inhabitant. In it, she belonged to him totally. He even denied her a mirror so she could not see her own face and affirm her own identity. However, she found in her struggle to fight back a curious sense of liberation. Since her abduction, she had stopped wetting the bed.

In a further move to make her his own, Priklopil decided that Natascha should change her name to Maria. She did not mind as she had never really liked the name Natascha anyway. Maria was her middle name anyway and both her grandmothers had been called Maria.

On a moonlit night in December 1999, he warned her not to cry out and took her out into the garden. She did as she was told as he made it clear that any attempt to escape would be met by death.

Eventually, she awoke one morning to find that she was having her first period. After Priklopil came to the cellar, he went to buy sanitary towels she had seen advertised on the TV. From then on, if she came upstairs when she was having her period, he forced her to sit on a pile of newspapers. The tiniest spot of blood might render tell-tale DNA. Then, as his paranoia grew, she had to wear a plastic bag over her hair. Any stray hair found around the house was burnt. Later, he shaved her head.

Now that she was on the verge of womanhood, he stopped treating her as a child and gave her what he considered housewifely chores around the house. While she was upstairs, the blinds were kept down. The house itself was screened by shrubbery, and it was located in a quiet backstreet where there were few passers-by. The only noise came from the nearby train line to Vienna.

While she was upstairs during the day, he watched her all the time. He would stand behind her giving orders as she cleaned. She needed permission to sit down or stand up; she could not even go to the toilet alone. Later, he took off the lavatory door so he could watch her. The only time she had to herself was when she was returned to the dungeon at night.

Priklopil was an admirer of Hitler and a follower of Austria's far-right Freedom Party. The 9/11 attack on the

World Trade Center was a cause for celebration, he said, as New York was the centre of the Jewish conspiracy for world domination. Rather than feeling contempt, Natasha took pity on him. She addressed him affectionately as 'Wolfgang' or even 'Wolfi', but she had refused to call him 'Master'. He then insisted that she kneel in front of him and call him 'My Lord'. When she would not do that either, she was beaten.

Shortly before he had abducted Natascha, Priklopil had lost his job at the electronics firm Siemens. While living on unemployment benefit, he and Ernst Holzapfel made extra money renovating apartments. Priklopil now decided to divide his own house into apartments. Although she was still only 12, she had to help him in strenuous building work. He often lost his temper and beat her, although he apologized afterwards. Later, she began to hit back, but she was no match for him physically and suffered with worse beatings.

To keep her weak and submissive, he cut her rations, saying she was getting fat. She found herself constantly hungry and suffered stomach cramps at night. Bald and emaciated, he made her work nearly naked as she would be less likely to run out into the street that way. The only relief came at the weekends. When his mother came, he would lock her in her dungeon. She would eat the three days' rations of food he left for her on the Friday night so once a week she would have a full belly.

As well as making the house spotlessly clean for his mother's arrival, Natascha also had to follow the recipes she had been left to the letter. But no matter what she did, he said that the result was never as good as his mother's.

When she was 14, he let her stay above ground at night.

He would lock her in his bedroom with him, with her hands tied to his so she could not get away. Jealous of her privacy, Natascha has refused to talk about what went on in the bedroom, but she has said that she was subjected to minor sexual assaults as part of her daily humiliation. Speculation was fuelled by *Stern* magazine which discovered that Priklopil was known to be active in the S&M scene in Vienna.

In the summer, Priklopil let Natascha go out into the garden to sunbathe and, when the neighbours were away, he took her for a swim in their pool. But this was followed by a dark period for the teenager. He beat her, starved her and kept her for long periods in the dark in the cellar while chanting, 'Obey! Obey! Obey!' down the intercom.

Natascha followed the trial of Marc Dutoux on the television. Sabine Dardenne's cell had been even smaller than her own, but now she was confronting her abductor in court. The Dutroux case sparked new interested in girls who had disappeared, but she heard on the radio that the authorities had given up looking for her long ago and it was assumed that she was dead.

Natascha had already tried to commit suicide twice by trying to strangle herself and, on another occasion, slitting her wrists. Both attempts had failed. This time she put paper on the hot plate, hoping her cell would fill up with smoke and suffocate her. But when she began to cough uncontrollably, she doused the smouldering paper. In the morning, Priklopil beat her black and blue.

One day, she asked if he could open a window. Accusing her of trying to escape, he dragged her to the front, opened it and said, 'Just see how far you get, the way you look.'

She was barely dressed, her body was bruised and emaciated, her hair was cropped and she lost her nerve. On another occasion, he flung her outside naked. Again, she could not flee. If he caught her, he would kill her; he said he would also kill any neighbour she ran to. She would be responsible for that. Her parents were in jail, he said, so she could not go home. In the end, she begged to be let back into the house.

Priklopil believed that he had her so completely in his thrall that he decided to take her out in his van. He let her hair grow back, then bleached it blonde. If questioned, she was to say that she was his niece. It was the first time she had been out of the house in seven years.

In a small wood just outside town, he let her get out of the van, briefly. Afterwards, they went out to a chemist where she was allowed to buy something for herself. But she was warned not to say a word or he would kill everyone in the shop. However, she exchanged a few innocent words with a shop assistant. When they got home, he beat her remorselessly. Next time they went out, she promised herself she would find the strength to ask someone for help.

The opportunity came one morning what he took her to a do-it-yourself store. On the way, they passed her grandmother's house; they also passed the turning to the apartment block where she had lived with her mother. The good times she had spent with her grandma seemed a lifetime away. Tears filled her eyes as they passed the turning to the apartment where she had lived with her mother; her sister's apartment was also nearby. Noticing the welling tears, Priklopil ordered her to keep her eyes on the floor.

In the DIY store, Natascha looked for someone she could

turn to for help, but everyone seemed self-absorbed and unfriendly. Then a sales assistant asked, 'Can I help you?'

'No thanks,' said Priklopil. 'We're fine.'

That night, she rued missing another opportunity to break free. Somehow, she would have to build up the strength. In the secret diary she used to keep a record of the beatings, she wrote a list of instructions to herself. She must not react to the things he did to undermine her self-confidence. She told herself that she must be stronger; most of all, she must never give up.

On the next outing, they were stopped at a police checkpoint. This was a perfect opportunity to escape. But if she jumped out of the car and sought help from the police, Priklopil might take off and crash into the oncoming traffic. The police officer said his papers were in order and handed them back.

Another opportunity had been lost, and although this plunged her back into despair she realized that she was gradually moving in the right direction. At first, she had spent all her effort getting out of the cellar, then she had aimed to get out of the house; both of those goals had been achieved. What she had to do now was escape his controlling influence. When they went out, she could feel him shaking and she realized that he was torn between wanting to live a seemingly normal life with her and the fear that she would destroy everything by escaping. This was a conflict that she could exploit.

As Natascha approached her 18th birthday, Priklopil suggested taking her on a skiing trip. When he took her to buy some ski pants, she could, at last, see herself in a mirror. She was so pitifully thin she had to get ski pants from a children's store. Although the trip had been his suggestion, Priklopil then began to blame Natascha for the expense. Despite all the money he was spending, he said, she would probably spoil everything by acting up, screaming, 'You're nothing without me.' She did not respond; she had already written in her secret diary, 'Don't answer back when he says that you can't live without him.'

Priklopil had gone skiing before, leaving her in the cellar. She realized that she was going along to play the willing partner who admired his prowess on the slopes. Playing on this, as they set off, she said she had changed her mind and wanted to stay at home. He hit her with a crowbar.

At the ski rental shop where Natascha was to get some boots, she would have to talk to the assistant. Again, he warned her that he would kill everyone in the shop if she tried to give him away. The whole exercise made him so nervous that he decided that they could not take the ski lift as it would give her another chance to talk to people. Instead, they drove up to the slopes.

Her first attempts at skiing met with some success, which boosted her confidence. Priklopil, of course, nit-picked – but it just seemed petty when confronted with the vastness of the sky and the mountainous panorama. When she needed to go to the lavatory, he directed her to a restroom away from the restaurant area where there were fewer people, and he stood outside the door. There was no one inside, but she delayed until someone came in. At first, she thought it was Priklopil, then she saw it was a woman. For the first time in eight years, Natascha found herself alone with someone else rather than her kidnapper.

Natascha plucked up all her courage and spoke to the

stranger. She did not react, washed her hands, smiled at Natascha and left. Later, she learned that the woman was Dutch and did not understand German. It was like a nightmare where you open your mouth and nothing comes out. Another chance to escape had been lost and Natascha went home with Priklopil feeling utterly devastated.

As a treat, Natascha was allowed to bake a cake for her 18th birthday. This was the age, even before she had been abducted, that she had planned to move out of the family home. There was no party. Instead, she had to watch videos of Turkish and Serbian wedding celebrations that Priklopil had bought and wondered where this was leading. He also bought her a second cake in the shape of a '1' and an '8'. The '18' made her redouble her resolve to escape. She was no longer a child and, despite what he said, she did not need anyone looking after her any more. Back in her dungeon, she thought of the ambitions she had had as a little girl – she had wanted to write a book, be an actress, make music … be free.

After her birthday, she was allowed outside to help with the gardening. The neighbours saw her, and even shouted greetings over the fence. Priklopil had told them that she was his temporary help. He even bought her an orange dress which made her feel almost normal.

The conversion work on the house was finished and they then had started work on an apartment he had bought in Vienna. Again, Natascha was an unpaid labourer. The hope was that being away from the dungeon would present her with new opportunities. However, if he left the apartment for even a moment, he jammed the door closed or screwed boards across it, turning the flat into a makeshift prison. The sad fact was that she was usually too weak from overwork and her poor diet to make a break for it.

An opportunity to escape did present itself when a neighbour came round from an adjoining apartment, but he was a Yugoslav and spoke little German. While Priklopil talked to him in the doorway, he made sure he kept Natascha behind him. Nevertheless, she was sure that the opportunity to escape would present itself eventually. Meanwhile, there were fresh beatings. If he said that black was white, she was forced to agree. And he was becoming more delusional. He talked of taking her away on holiday and buying her nice things, but when she promised not to try and escape, he said she was lying.

There were other worries. She had been with him for so long she wondered whether she would be able to cope with freedom and feared she might commit suicide. And she had no desire to involve the police – they would lock him up. Although that was exactly what Priklopil had done to her, she had no appetite for revenge. She only felt pity for a man who thought he could force someone to love him.

Neither did Natascha want to be presented as a victim as the girls in the Dutroux case had been. Once she was free of Priklopil, she wanted her 'victim' status to be over. She may have been a child when she had disappeared into the cellar, but she would emerge as a fully grown woman and she even planned how she would handle the media.

As work on the apartment drew to a close, Priklopil's mood lightened. Once it had been sold, his money worries would be over. He also planned to sell the white van he had used to kidnap her eight-and-a-half years earlier. While they were getting it ready for sale, Natascha realized that her last link to the world before her abduction was about to disappear. In her mind, it was as if she was condemning herself to the cellar for ever. This prompted her to speak out. She told Priklopil that she was now an adult and wanted to move out. He must have known from the beginning that, sooner or later, he would either have kill her or let her go. She expected him to hit her. Instead, he said that he could neither kill her nor free her. But Natascha insisted that he had put them in a position where the only way out was for one of them to die. She had already tried to kill herself several times, but she said it would be better if he committed suicide.

Again, she showed compassion for her kidnapper. He was not to worry, she said. If she ran away, she would not go to the police. Instead, she would throw herself under a train. She surprised herself when she said this, but now she knew that she would run away at the next opportunity.

On the morning of 23 August 2006, she awoke when the light came on. As usual, hunger drove her out of bed. There was no food in the cellar. She had had no dinner the night before and she had eaten the tiny piece of cake he had given her for her breakfast instead. All she could do was brush her teeth to take away the sour taste of her empty stomach. Her usual daily routine was to tidy up her cell, but she could not be bothered that morning. She put on her new orange dress and waited for her jailer to open the door.

She asked Priklopil whether she could put on a pair of panties. This, he said, was out of the question. Just as she had always had to work nearly naked indoors to deter her from escaping, in the garden she had to go without underwear. It was a day like any other day. She shuddered as she passed through the big concrete door. Long before, she had used her last ounce of strength to smash down the inner wooden door when he had left her alone for a several of days. But when she came up against the concrete door, she gave up. It could only be opened from the outside. If something prevented him coming to open it, she would have died from thirst or starvation. This had preyed on her mind for years.

After that, there was the long crawl along the narrow passageway. Once upstairs, she took deep breaths of cool, fresh air. Even though Natascha was starving, she had to get her captor two slices of bread and jam from the kitchen. There would be none for her. Afterwards, she did the washing up, and she looked at the calendar. It was the 3,096th day of her captivity.

They wrote an advertisement for the apartment and put it on the Internet, then went out into the garden. Around noon, Priklopil told her to vacuum the inside of the van, ready for a buyer. While she was doing that, his cell phone rang. From what she overheard of the conversation, someone was interested in the apartment. While talking, Priklopil wandered away.

As soon as he was out of sight, Natascha seized her chance. She dropped the vacuum cleaner and ran. With no clear idea of where to go, she headed towards the railroad tracks that led back to Vienna. She did not even believe that she would get away; Priklopil would inevitably catch up with her and kill her. Even so, she now felt that death was better than returning to the dungeon. She saw three people in the street and begged them to call the police. They said they could not help as none of them had a cell phone with them. In frustration, she began to cry.

Eager to get off the street, she climbed over a fence into a garden. A woman was just opening a window. Natascha asked her to call the police, but the woman wanted to know what Natascha was doing in her garden. Natascha again begged her to call the police. She had been kidnapped. Then she added, 'My name is Natascha Kampusch.'

For Natascha, this broke the spell. For the first time in many years, she was no longer Priklopil's little Maria. In that instant, she had reclaimed her own name. Fearing a bloodbath, she told the woman that the police should come in an unmarked car. Even so, the woman was still mistrustful and told Natascha to wait by the hedge – she did not want her on her lawn. Nevertheless, she called the police.

The message about sending an unmarked vehicle had not got through and a police car turned up with its lights flashing. Natascha feared that gunfire would break out any moment, as did the police, who told her to put her hands up.

Natascha told them her name, her date of birth and her mother's address. The police were not convinced. This emaciated teenager before them looked nothing like the plump primary-school girl who had gone missing eight-and-a-half years earlier.

While they contacted headquarters, she said that she had been held prisoner at Heinestrasse 60. She also warned them that her kidnapper, Wolfgang Priklopil, was only yards away and they were in great danger.

The police put Natascha in the car and she ducked down low in the back seat, terrified that Priklopil might see her. As they made their way to the police station at Deutsch-Wagram, detectives came to interview her. When they arrived, they greeted her warmly. They had checked out the details she had given and were convinced that she was the lost child they have given up searching for long ago. They offered her some food. Wisely, she refused it, knowing that a sudden surfeit of food would give her stomach cramps. A kindly woman police officer wrapped Natascha in her jacket to keep her warm, then sat her down so that she could pour out her story. Then she was taken back to Vienna where she was mobbed by the media. It was then that she heard that Priklopil was on the run. She knew he would kill himself.

Her mother was waiting at police headquarters, then her sisters and her father turned up. But her beloved grandmother in Strasshof, sadly, had died. Next, she had an appointment with police psychologist.

Meanwhile, detectives examined Heinsestrasse 60. There were no explosives around the doors and windows as Priklopil had threatened. But, this time, they did find the dungeon.

With Priklopil still at large, the police took Natascha to a hotel in southern Austria under armed guard. They feared that Priklopil might try and kill her so, once again, Natascha found herself locked up. She turned to the radio to see if she could find out what had happened to her kidnapper, but the psychologist put a stop to this. The next day, when she was on the way back to Vienna, she was told that Priklopil had jumped in front of a train and was dead. At least now she would not have to relive her ordeal at a trial.

Natascha Kampusch was advised to change her name and go into hiding. It was the only way she could lead a normal life, she was told. But Natascha refused to live in the shadows. She had disappeared once before and she was not doing it again.

Two weeks after her escape, Natascha began giving

interviews to the major Austrian news media, and she went on to have her own chat show on Austrian TV.

After the death of Priklopil, she was awarded possession of the house at Heinestrasse and chose to keep it for herself, preventing it from being turned into some macabre museum, or torn down. She had spent so many years there, the place had become extremely important to her. Since her escape, she has visited it regularly, but says that if she ever sold it, she would first have the cellar filled in.

22

A RESCUE
IN RUSSIA

Nobody knows how many people worldwide vanish off the streets and disappear into captivity. No one knew that this was the fate of Michelle Knight, Amanda Berry and Gina DeJesus until they emerged in 2013. The world had already been shocked by the stories of Natascha Kampusch and Elisabeth Fritzl; their emergence had prompted the media to seek out similar cases – including one in Russia.

As with Ariel Castro, the captives were young girls – 17-year-old student Lena Simakina and her 14-year-old friend, schoolgirl Katya Martynova, who lived in the Ryazan Oblast, some 150 miles south of Moscow.

On 30 September 2000, there was a party at a disco in Sobornaya Square in the centre of the city of Ryazan to celebrate the Russian Orthodox holiday of *Vera, Nadezhda and Lyubov* – Faith, Hope and Love. On their way home, they accepted a lift home from 48-year-old Viktor Mokhov, an unemployed former metalworker at the Skopin car factory, and his girlfriend, 25-year-old Yelena Badukina, who introduced herself as 'Lyosha'. Like Colleen Stan, the girls figured they were safe because there was a woman in the car.

In the Lada, the two girls were plied with vodka that had been laced with sedatives. They awoke in a dungeon. It was 9ft underground and their screams could not be heard by anyone outside. As far as the outside world was concerned, they had disappeared.

Ex-army officer Mokhov had been planning this for some time. The underground cell, which measured 8ft by 10ft, had taken three years to excavate. He dug out some 60 tons of earth by hand, spreading it on his allotment nearby. Like Jamelske's and Priklopil's dungeons, it was hidden under his ramshackle garage, but could not be accessed directly from it. The entrance was hidden to one side and screened from the garden by a wooden fence.

A steel door 6in (15cm) thick was hidden by a thin metal plate held in place by magnets. This had to be prized back with a screwdriver. Behind the steel door was a small room just 3ft high at ground level. In the floor, there was a trapdoor. Once it was opened, a wooden ladder led to another chamber below. In it was a padlocked steel hatch at ankle height that measured just 20in by 15in (50cm by 38cm). It was so small that Mokhov could barely squeeze through it.

Beyond yet another door was the girls' cell and the entrance to the 'sex chamber' where Mokhov repeatedly raped them. There were ventilation holes in the concrete ceiling and an electric light. He also provided a small electric cooker where the girls could cook rice to supplement the inadequate rations he gave them. He also lowered two buckets – one to be used as a lavatory, the other containing water for washing.

Mokhov demanded sex every day. If the girls refused, he beat them with a rubber hose. There were other punishments; if they tried to resist, he would starve them or cut off their electricity leaving them in the dark and the cold in the Russian winter. He could also limit their supply of air to the point of near-suffocation, or sprayed tear gas into the cellar to induce panic.

Once they had been forced to give in to his sexual demands, he would take them through into the smaller room. The walls had been decorated with pictures from pornographic magazines and he would act out his fantasies with them. For the younger girl, Katya, this brutal, humiliating experience at the hands of a monster was her first introduction to sex. 'I was a virgin when I went in there,' she said. 'It was my first time. Just think how that makes me feel. He ruined something that should have been so special for me.'

No one else in Skopin knew that Lena and Katya were missing, nor did they know that Mokhov was a sex offender, although this was not his first offence and one person at least knew about his dungeon. In December 1999, he had plied a 16-year-old girl and her boyfriend with alcohol, then made advances towards the girl. When she refused him and left, he followed her out into the street, hit her over the head and dragged her back to his bunker. For two weeks, he kept her in the dungeon and repeatedly raped her. She managed to escape, but she did not report the incident and Mokhov remained free to strike again.

He had also learned a lesson and tightened security. There was no chance of escape for Lena and Katya. 'We tried everything to get away,' said Katya. The only way out, they decided was to murder Mokhov. 'We tried to kill him once, a month after we were kidnapped,' she said. 'We attacked him and tried to strangle him with a heater cord. But he threw it off his neck.'

When force failed, the abused girls tried to persuade him to let them go, assuring him of their silence. 'We promised him we wouldn't go to the police,' said Katya. 'And we meant it.' But Mokhov was unmoved. Like Gary Heidnik, he had bigger plans. 'He said, "I'll only let you go in 20 years, when each of you has given me ten babies."'

Lena's suffering parallels that of Amanda Berry and Elisabeth Fritzl. She gave birth twice underground with help only from Katya and a medical manual Mokhov had supplied. Under those circumstances, it was a miracle that mother and babies survived. 'The first boy, Vladik, was much healthier than the second, Oleg, who was small and blue, and did not cry,' said Katya. 'I was washing and cleaning the baby after tying up his tummy button and Lena collapsed on the bed. Could I ever imagine I would deliver two babies successfully? I don't know how I managed.'

After it was clear that the babies were going to live, Mokhov took them away and abandoned them in the entranceways to apartment blocks in the small town of Skopin. The two boys were found and sent to an orphanage.

Katya was terrified that she might fall pregnant, too. She prayed that she would not conceive and, if she did, she was determined not to carry the child to full term. 'Every day I would pray that I wouldn't be pregnant,' she said. 'If I had been, I would have exercised my stomach so hard that I aborted the baby.'

There was little to do in the dungeon except await the next sex attack. However, as time went on Mokhov's sexual demands tailed off to twice a week. He also tried to be nice to the girls, rewarding them with books, paints, pens and paper. They passed the time drawing and learning English. An exercise book found on the floor was filled with neat handwriting in blue ballpoint pen. One entry read, 'The remains of an extinct hippopotamus have been found by a party of Soviet and Mongolian palaeontologists.'

This was small comfort in the appalling conditions they were living under. The air was fetid and the walls were slimy and damp. Their furniture consisted of two bunk beds with mattresses that were mouldy, a small table and a stool. They decorated the walls of their living quarters with posters of Madonna and *Baywatch* star Pamela Anderson, along with a religious icon and a landscape showing a woman standing by a river painted by Katya. She also built a matchstick castle, which she took with her when she left the cellar.

Like Michelle Knight and Gina DeJesus, they depended on each other. 'There were two bunk beds, but we slept together,' said Katya. 'At the beginning, we just lay on it with our arms around each other and cried all the time. During the first six months, we were apathetic; we did nothing. It was only later that we started making our bed, cooking, keeping busy. We needed to make our life as bearable as we could to survive.'

This gave them hope, though death never seemed far away. 'Katya and I prayed every day,' said Lena. 'We never gave up. We lived in fear of death but still hoped. We wanted to believe that one day he'd let us go, though he said, "Why should I? It is easier to kill you." But we planned it anyway. We always had a note ready with our addresses and what had happened to us. We tried to hide notes in the clothes of my second son but that bastard must have found them all.'

Neither did they reconcile themselves to being Mokhov's sex slaves. 'He was a cruel, poisonous, sly, stupid coward – cruelty and cowardice were his nature,' said Katya. 'Contact with him was the worst thing. He was old, smelly and so ugly. I don't think either of us got used to it.'

The girls showed extraordinary spirit. They began exercising every day, while Katya wrote poems and read. The boredom was relieved somewhat when, on 1 May 2001, Mokhov bought them a small black-and-white TV set. 'We watched it for hours on end,' Katya said. 'We even watched the ads with the same excitement.' And, even better, it gave them hope when they saw Sabine Dardenne on TV after being freed from Marc Dutroux's dungeon in Belgium. 'We saw her smiling and saying she wouldn't let this experience ruin her life in the future,' said Lena. 'I remember turning to Katya and crying, like we did hundreds of times. I remember asking, "Will we ever give interviews and smile like this?"'

Later, Mokhov bought them a tape recorder. It was to be his undoing.

Mokhov began boasting to drinking companions about the 'mini-harem' under his garage. No one really believed him, as Mokhov was not known as a lothario. He had been married once in the 1970s, but it had only lasted three months before he returned home to his mother, Alisa

Mokhova, who was now 80. However, some people became suspicious because his mother seemed to be buying too much food for just the two of them.

Occasionally, he let the girls go up to the trapdoor and smell the air. Towards the end of their captivity, he became confident enough to allow them outside after dark to exercise one at a time. And he had an ulterior motive; he wanted them to help him seduce a young female student who had moved into the house as a lodger. Katya was introduced to the target as a relative and, while she made her acquaintance, she was able to slip the girl an audio-cassette tape and asked her to give it to the police. Inside, there was a note that said, 'This person knows where we are.'

The police had long since given up finding the two girls and had assumed they were dead. But on 26 April 2004, prompted by the note, they went to Mokhov's home and found them. The girls were in a shocking condition. After being deprived of sunlight for 1,320 days, starved and abused, they were extremely weak. Lena found she could not walk more than a few yards without help. Her skin was light green and she smelled of mould.

When she was released, Lena was eight months' pregnant but, due to her poor state of health, the child was stillborn. And she suffered a dilemma over her two other children. 'When they were inside me, I didn't think of them as my children,' she said. 'They were his babies, implanted against my will.' Even so, she could not suppress her maternal instincts. When she was rescued, her first words were, 'Please, please find my babies and bring them back to me.'

Later, she changed her mind. After six weeks of freedom,

she said, 'I don't want to see them now, because I know I will only cry and get distressed. They will always remind me of him and that's not best for them. They deserve the chance of a decent life and I don't know if I'm strong enough to give them what they need.'

Mokhov was unrepentant. He told investigators, 'I wanted to have many children. I wanted to improve the demographic situation of Russia.' He was sentenced to 17 years in a labour camp, plus two years in jail. It hardly seemed enough. 'Nothing is enough for him,' said Lena.

Yelena Badukina was jailed for 15 years, though little is known of her motive. No charges were laid against Mokhov's mother and it is generally assumed that she did not know what her son was up to.

When Lena was abducted, she had a boyfriend. But, thinking her dead, he married another woman. However, in 2004, Katya introduced her to Dima Isaev and, less than two years after she had been released, they married in a Georgian ceremony. 'I thought it was utterly impossible that I'd ever be able to love or even trust a man,' said Lena. 'My wedding day felt like a miracle. It was as if I was watching a film. When I was in the cellar, I stopped dreaming of the future. I didn't think I would ever get out. I thought I would die down there and never love again. If I'd imagined having someone to love me, I would have gone crazy. Instead, I focused purely on survival. I knew which thoughts it was safe to have and which ones were too painful to cope with ... It still seems surreal that I have a normal life ahead of me.'

By then, she had secured a place at university to study journalism and planned to start a family. 'I would like two or three,' she said.

Lena sent a message to Natascha Kampusch when she was freed. 'My message to Natascha is private, for her only,' she said. 'I hope it will help her with what lies ahead. Back then, I never would have thought that I could have a normal life ahead of me. I thought I would never love or even trust a man, so when my family and friends toasted us at our wedding last year it felt like a miracle. But when I had been locked in the cellar, I had given up all hope and stopped dreaming. It was all I could do to survive.'

Another message was forthcoming from Lena and Katya when Elisabeth Fritzl was released. 'We want to tell Elisabeth, it can be all right,' they said. 'Not all men are monsters. You can find true love, as we have. We know something of what you went through and will go through in the future as you try to recover.'

Indeed, it was reported that, while convalescing, Elisabeth had fallen in love with one of her guards. Katya added, 'Elisabeth, please know you will recover and you will learn to trust again. Love can conquer anything, however horrific. Our lesson is that you can put all this ordeal somewhere at the back of your mind and get on and live a completely new life.'

It is a message of hope that should go to all those who have disappeared and, miraculously, re-entered the world.